The Yogi

Praise for *The Yogi*

"I consider myself very lucky to have studied yoga in the mid-sixties with Swami Vishnu-devananda. You could feel his unique and charismatic energy the moment he entered the room. This book captures that energy. It will inspire as well as bring great enthusiasm to your own spiritual pathway."

—LILIAS FOLAN
Lilias Yoga Complete

"Swami Vishnu-devananda was a living example of the power of faith. Whenever I think of him I am reminded of the Children of Israel fleeing from Egypt, blocked by the Red Sea. They didn't know what to do. They didn't want to go back and be slaves, but they couldn't swim across the sea. When Moses asked God what they should do, God said that they should simply go forward, plunge in, and everything would be taken care of. That is how Swami Vishnu taught me to approach my life. Don't worry about tomorrow. Just press on, doing what you know is right. This book shows Swamiji for what he was: a simple, energetic man full of love for his fellow man and moved by his faith in God to spread the knowledge of yoga throughout the world."

—RABBI JOSEPH GELBERMAN

"Some men are called to challenge society to a higher vision. Vishnu-devananda was such a man. He accepted the enormous burden of teaching an aggressive world with an indominable energy of peace and wisdom. The remembrances in these pages puts one in touch with his irresistible spirit. This book is dynamic and inspirational reading at its finest!"

—YOGI ACHALA

"It is with great love and appreciation that I remember my brother monk, our beloved Swami Vishnu-devananda. He is not easily forgotten! A great and accomplished hatha yogi, he was one of the first swamis to come to the West and impart the great teachings of yoga science to eager students here. Through the many teaching and retreat centers that Swamiji established around the world, sincere seekers were introduced to yoga and the message of Swami Sivananda Maharaj. Swami Vishnu-devananda was not an ordinary sanyasin. All of us who knew him when he entered the Rishikesh Ashram knew he would achieve great things and be a beacon of divine light. He had a great and novel universal vision that was only limited by the confines of his physical form. Now he has shed that burden in order to be free to continue his service unimpeded. May his noble vision be perpetuated and flourish in the hearts of all his devotees. "

—SWAMI SATCHIDANANDA
Founder, Integral Yoga Society

The Yogi

Portraits of Swami Vishnu-devananda

Gopala Krishna

Yes International Publishers
Saint Paul, Minnesota

Yes International Publishers
1317 Summit Avenue, St. Paul, MN 55105-2602
Phone: 612-645-6808

Library of Congress Cataloging-in-Publication Data

Krishna, Gopala, 1949-
The yogi : portraits of Swami Vishnu-devananda /
Gopala Krishna
    p.   cm.
ISBN 0-936663-12-X (paperback)
1. Vishnudevananda, Swami.
2. Yogis — India — Biography.
3. Hindus — India — Biography.   I. Title.
BL 1175. V4775K75   1995
294.5'092—dc20   95-4692
    [b]   CIP

Printed in the United States of America.

Contents

Preface

The original idea for this book was not mine. Soon after Swami Vishnu-devananda, or as he was usually called by his students and friends, Swamiji, had his first stroke early in 1991, one of his senior disciples, Swami Shankarananda, sent out a request to Swamiji's students to send in material for a book. He made a start at gathering and collating the information that flowed in, as well as starting to transcribe the thousands of tapes of Swamiji's talks that are in the Sivananda Yoga Ashram archives. Swami Shankarananda's hectic schedule and many other responsibilities made it impossible for him to get very far into the project.

In the first few days after Swamiji left his body, November 9th, 1993, it became clear to me that I should take on this project myself. I cannot explain or describe how this feeling arose. It was just there, full blown. I'd never written anything larger than a short scientific paper on some aspect of computer technology, but I knew I could write this book. What I wanted to do was to somehow preserve and pass on what Swamiji taught all of us over the years.

I immersed myself in the material that had been collected, and set about gathering more. Every day was filled with thoughts, images and memories of Swamiji. As I read transcripts of his talks I could often see and hear him very clearly in my mind. It was like being with him again, sitting at his feet. Hopefully as you read this book, you too will feel his presence.

Swamiji guided me through the whole process. He wrote this book. I have only acted as his instrument. I don't mean to imply by this that I have some sort of special relationship with Swamiji; many of his thousands of students could have written this book. I just got lucky.

The chapters in this book are arranged partly in chronological order, as you would find in a biography, and partly by topic. The biographical chapters are in part based on an autobiographical tape about his early life that Swami Vishnu-devananda made in the mid 1980's. The topical chapters contain something Swamiji said about that subject during *satsang*. Luckily, many of his talks were recorded, either on audio or video tape, so I had a vast collection of his own thoughts and teaching to draw from. Interspersed with this material drawn directly from Swamiji will be a selection of memories of people who knew him.

To help the reader follow who is speaking, this book delineates the sections with various type faces:

> Paragraphs taken from Swamiji's talks will appear in this format. He would regularly gather together everyone who was around him for *satsang*. We would sit and meditate and chant

mantras together and then Swamiji would talk, sometimes briefly, often at great length. For some of these talks the topic would be pre-planned, for instance when he was giving a particular course like the Teacher Training Course he taught regularly. At times he would open at random one of the books of his *guru*, Swami Sivananda, read a bit of what he found, and take off from there. From time to time the topic would arise out of what he read in the newspaper that day, or had seen on the TV news. Finally Swamiji would sometimes ask for questions during *satsang*, making sure that he dealt with an individual's questions and doubts on the spot, and at the same time offering a broader teaching to all of us.

Swamiji had a unique style. As much as possible I have kept the text of his talks verbatim. For clarity and brevity, I have edited out digressions and interruptions and corrected his not always perfect English. No effort has been made to delete what may at first seem to be repetitive sections. Swamiji would often repeat himself, making sure the message sunk in.

> Paragraphs of memories from Swamiji's students and friends will appear in this format. Part of what this book is trying to preserve is the more private and individual teaching he did with each and every one of us. He was a loving, caring human being who took personal interest in each and every person he came in contact with. These memories will hopefully reflect these more private and individual lessons.

Where several memories are printed together, one after another, the change from one person's story to another's will be indicated by this separator:

ॐ नमो नारायणाय

This Sanskrit mantra is transliterated in English script as *Om Namo Narayanaya*, and in translation means "Prostrations to Lord Vishnu." Vishnu is the divine preserver of the universe. Wherever Swamiji went he encouraged people to repeat, chant, and write this mantra. He said that by doing so we would invoke the preservative power of Lord Vishnu and help make the world a better, more peaceful place.

Acknowledgements

First and foremost I must thank all my brothers and sisters in the Sivananda Yoga Vedanta organization for all the help they gave me in gathering the material I used to write this book. Without their consistent input and encouragement, and the many wonderful memories of Swamiji they contributed, this book simply would not exist.

A few people gave me much needed technical help during this project, including David Dwyer, who translated all the original computer disks of information into a format I could use, and my friend Shelley Burke, who translated everything I received in Spanish into English.

I am grateful to *Yoga International* for publishing sections of this book in the November-December, 1994 edition.

Finally I owe a great deal to Theresa King for her guidance and knowledge, helping me take my original idea and bring it to its present, more coherent, form.

Introduction

This little book is a documentary compilation of primary autobiographical sources and reminiscences by disciples and friends from the life of the late "Flying-Swami," Swami Vishnu-devananda (1927 - 1993) of India and Canada, Hindu monk and pilot. Swami Vishnu was one of the twentieth century's most extraordinary activists for world peace and justice, non-violence, open borders, and the realization of the global citizenship of all humanity in what he called a "true world order" awaiting the spiritual maturation of our race.

Swami Vishnu was one of the most remarkable persons of our age on a number of fronts from the 1950's in Canada and around the world until the time of his death in India in 1993. He conceived and executed a stunning array of prophetic and symbolic events as part of his global peace mission on site in most of the world's major trouble spots. He was a leader in the Americas, Europe, the Caribbean, the Middle-East, India, and parts of Asia in the propagation of the knowledge of yoga vedanta, the practice of yoga for health, non-violence, inner and outer peace, and hidden potentials of the human soul and spirit for turning "the darkness into the light," to help our planet survive and to make our world a better place in which to live.

He was a close friend and for a number of years in the '70s and '80s he asked my assistance in arranging international conferences and events to call attention to the relevance of yoga (and the ancient cosmology, philosophy of life, and psychology upon which it is based) to emerging new sciences of consciousness, the new physics, the new medicine, new therapies, the growing planetary ecological consciousness. From my standpoint he understood the significance of our increased interest in the West in reports by many persons affirming human immortality after having various extraordinary psychic and spiritual experiences.

In one of the early events in which I participated in 1977, he led an unforgettable 45 day pilgrimage and lecture tour of India via Spain on the topic of "Yoga and Psychic Discoveries." This event featured a Hindu Swami (himself), a Christian priest (myself), a Psychic (Dr. Marilyn Rossner, my wife, a children's therapist and special educator, as well as a practicing yogi and gifted sensitive), and an Astronaut (Dr. Edgar Mitchell, who had performed a successful ESP experiment between his lunar capsule and the earth).

Swami Vishnu's consistent genius and flair for the imaginative and timely capture of public attention was deeply spiritually motivated. Wherever he went, he established ashrams and centers through which he was able to touch peoples' lives, change their lifestyles for the better, and increase the world's awareness of the urgent need for positive thinking, healthy living, a true spirituality and a dramatic improvement in human behaviors.

When he first arrived in North America from India via South Asia in 1957 as a young Hindu *sanyasin*, he had no money, no one to take him in, and precious little practical knowledge of Western ways or persuasive fluency in English, for that matter, to smooth his path.

What he did possess was a very bright, focused, dedicated, positive soul fashioned in its formative years by one of the greatest yoga adepts and sages of the Himalayas, Swami Sivananda of Rishikesh, a medical doctor and Hindu monk known to masses in that sub-continent as "the Saint Francis of Modern India." Sivananda was an important figure in the renaissance of Indian spirituality in the 19th and 20th centuries. Swami Vishnu also possessed the true spirit and inspiration of the Gandhian doctrine of nonviolent witness to peace and justice in places of urgent human suffering and need. These gifts and fruits of the spirit were his only required bank account and polish.

Swami Vishnu had a clear mandate to serve humanity from his teachers. He regarded this mandate to be from divinely inspired sources of inspiration. These sources and that inspiration never left him. He remained faithful to them with heroic determination through thick and thin until the day he left this world back in India, where his body was finally put into the sacred river Ganges. That mandate— in the very words of Sivananda—was one which Swamiji has emblazoned on the walls of all of his ashrams and centers for the spiritual formation of all of his students: "Serve, Love, Give, Purify, Meditate, Realize!"

His commission from his beloved *guru* Swami Sivananda was to live the philosophy and practice of yoga himself, and to teach it to his own disciples so that all could attain for themselves its goal: divine self-realization—the integration of body, mind, and spirit with the ground of being, God, Brahman, the Eternal Source of all life, health, joy, bliss—and the true inspiration and strength to walk in the *sanatana dharma*, the eternal, universal divine spiritual law.

Swami Vishnu was himself an authentic *guru* and a great spiritual teacher. He was very unprepossessing and humble in appearance. He would often shock disciples and guests by prostrating himself and asking forgiveness when he had been impatient, lost his temper, made mistakes, or offended anyone. He had a great love for people, but an impatience to get on with justice and intelligent courses of action as he perceived them. Wherever he perceived an individual in human need, or a great world tragedy, he wanted to race to the spot with aid, or some action of support, even when all he could do was to risk his life in some symbolic and prophetic action to call the attention of the rest of humanity to that need or tragedy.

You will learn in the following pages that he flew over the Arab-Israeli lines during the 1971 Mideast War in his small twin engine aircraft, "bombing" each side with flowers and peace leaflets: "Flowers, not Guns, to stop Wars!" He flew to Northern Ireland with the British comedian Peter Sellers to meet with Protestant and Catholic leaders. A Hindu Swami—brown skinned and wearing an orange cloth—affably lectured Christian leaders on the necessity for love, peace, and Christ-like action in a time of terror! He flew over the Berlin wall backwards into East Germany in an ultra-light aircraft, bearing the message to the East German police that, like the wall itself, all man-made barriers to peace dividing humanity could be transcended by the divine spirit operating within us. He then gave them a yoga lesson, a lecture on meditation; they fed him a cheese sandwich because he was a vegetarian, and gave him a subway token to travel back to West Berlin!

What Mahatma Ghandi did to inspire and to change the consciousness of the world was carried out almost entirely within the Indian sub-continent, with a brief period in South Africa. From that stage there went out to all parts of the globe the magnificent story of ahimsa, the principle of non-violence, and respect for the rights of all sentient life, and its inherent, gentle persuasive power eventually to bring racial and religious bigotry to an end.

What Swami Vishnu did in his lifetime for the same noble goal (although far less publicized), was in fact carried out on a much wider world stage in many continents and nations in a most spectacular way. He arranged an inspired series of unbelievable, symbolic, prophetic events spanning the last four decades of this century. Someday—when humanity has grown a bit and expanded its understanding of what is really newsworthy—there will undoubtedly be a major biographical book and film produced on the life of this unsung hero of our age. Until then, here is a sourcebook of reminiscences by his friends and disciples that communicates what he taught to the world.

Rev. John Rossner, O.Tr., Ph.D.
Professor of Comparative Religion & Culture
Concordia University, Montreal
President, International Institute of Integral Human Sciences

Chronology of the Life of Swami Vishnu-devananda

1927	Dec. 31	Born in Kannimangalam, Kerala, South India.
1928	June	Annaprashana (first feeding) and Nama Karana (naming) ceremonies at Palani Temple. Named Swamy Kuttan Nair.
1943		Passed high school exams. Teaches school briefly.
1944		Joins the army.
1945		Finds *Sadhana Tattwa* by Swami Sivananda in a garbage can. Visits Sivananda *Ashram* in Rishikesh for the first time.
1946		Returns for a brief visit to the *ashram* and realizes that Swami Sivananda is his *guru*. Discharged from the army and returns home to Kerala. Enters teachers college.
1947	Sept. 1	Arrives at Sivananda *Ashram* to attend Sivananda's diamond jubilee celebrations. Sivananda tells him to stay. He does.
1949	March	Initiated into *sanyas* as Swami Vishnu-devananda. Becomes Sivananda's personal assistant and the ashram's professor of yoga.
1950		Spends a year wandering as a penniless monk.
1952-53		Goes on All-India Tour with Sivananda.
1957	March	Sivananda sends him to go to the West where "people are waiting." He takes a long trip through the Pacific Rim area, earning his keep by teaching yoga classes, always moving one step closer to North America.
1957	Dec.	Arrives in San Francisco. Starts teaching classes there.
1958	July	Earns money by being a guinea pig at UCLA. Heads East for New York. Teaches classes in New York, but eventually has to move to Montreal.

1959		Establishes first yoga center in Montreal.
1960		First yoga camp for three weeks at a students summer cottage north of Montreal. Publishes *Complete Illustrated Book of Yoga*.
1962		Buys current Sivananda Yoga Camp property in Val Morin, with help from students. Starts his first ashram.
1963	July 14	Swami Sivananda dies.
1964	Sept.	Current New York City center opens.
1967		Establishes Sivananda *Ashram* Yoga Retreat on Paradise Island in the Bahamas.
1969	Winter	Has vision of world being engulfed in flames and people fleeing in all directions. Starts plans for world peace missions.
1969	Aug.	Holds first Teacher Training Course. Teaching centers opened in Chicago and Ft. Lauderdale, FL.
1970		Peter Max paints peace plane. Centers established in London and Washington.
1971	July 16	Krishna Temple inaugurated in Val Morin.
1971	Aug. 29	Opens Yoga Farm in Grass Valley, CA.
1971	Sept.-Oct.	Flies on world peace mission "bombing" Belfast, the Suez canal, Jerusalem, Lahore, and Bangladesh with flowers and leaflets.
1972-1976		Opens centers in Toronto, Vienna, Los Angeles, New Zealand, Munich, Geneva, Madrid, and Montevideo and the Sivananda Yoga Ranch in Woodbourne, NY.
1977		Organizes and holds three separate but related symposia, "Man and his Future" in Marbella, Spain, "Yoga and Psychic Discoveries" in Bangalore, India and "Physics and Metaphysics" in Los Angeles and New York.
1978		Publishes *Meditation and Mantras*. Opens *Ashram* in Neyyar Dam near Trivandrum, Kerala, India.
1978	July	Begins one year of silence.

1979	July	Breaks his silence. Holds Festival of Inner Light in Val Morin.
1981		Starts SAMA, Sivananda *Ashram* Members Association, a community of householder disciples next to the Val Morin *ashram*.
1983	Sept.	Flies over the Berlin Wall in an ultralight aircraft. Leads a firewalking ceremony next to the wall, with over 60 disciples participating.
1984	Jan.	Tours India with students in a double decker bus and land rover, trying to reawaken the spirit of yoga in India.
1984	Feb.	Attempts to mediate between Sikh nationalists and the Indian government by meeting with Sant Longowal and Sant Brindawal in the Golden Temple, Amritsar.
1986	Nov.	Begins six months in his cave at Gangotri, near the source of the Ganges River, high in the Himalayas. Suffers severe frostbite to his toes. Diagnosed as diabetic.
1987	Sept.	Leads All India Tour and Peace Mala, as part of Swami Sivananda's centennial celebrations. Opens Om Namo Narayanaya "Bank" on the top of a mountain opposite his cave in Gangotri, "depositing" thousands of pages of *likita japa* (mantra writing) gathered from students.
1991	Jan.	Has stroke that paralyses his left side.
1991	June	Kidneys fail. Starts daily dialysis treatments.
1991	Sept.	Returns to India and stays in his cave at Gangotri, receiving dialysis treatments while he is there.
1991	Dec.	Returns to Val Morin.
1992	July	Chooses site for new temple on top of hill overlooking the *ashram* in Val Morin.
1992	Sept.	Returns to India for Ganga Parigrama, a pilgrimage along the Ganges from its source 15,000 feet up in the Himalayas at Gomukh to where it enters the ocean.
1993	July	Inaugurates site of new temple by installing deities directly on the bare rock where the temple will be built.
1993	Oct.	Returns to India for Devi Temple pilgrimage.

1993   Nov. 1   Seriously ill. Taken to hospital in Manipal, India.

1993   Nov. 9   Mahasamadhi, final liberation from the body.

1993   Nov. 11   Jalasamadhi, immersion in the Ganges.

First Meetings

Swami Vishnu-devananda was born on December 31, 1927, in Kannimangalam, a small village in Kerala, South India. He was named Swamy Kuttan Nair. His family owned land in and around the village. He grew up living the simple village life of rural South India. Even today you cannot reach his first home in a motor vehicle. You have to stop on the main road and walk along the dike path, surrounded by rice patties, banana plantations, and tropical growth of all kinds. When I visited, the only "vehicle" I saw in the village was an elephant.

Growing up surrounded by the beauties of nature, the young boy's first spiritual lessons and struggles came while walking the four miles to and from school.

In my childhood, when I used to go to the school, I had to walk through many paddy fields. There were water snakes en route and their staple diet is frogs from the rice fields. These water snakes are not poisonous. My idea about religion and God started by watching the drama between life and death that exists between the frog and the water snake. Almost every day I would see a water snake catching a frog, most generally from the hind portion of the frog's body. Because the snake is unable to swallow the whole frog at once, the frog cries for several minutes in the mouth of the snake. The snake's mouth is so small it can't swallow all of the frog at once and the cry of the frog in his death pain can be heard for miles.

As I passed by, seeing the snake with the frog in his mouth, the realization would come, "That frog is now in the mouth of the snake, about to be swallowed, probably in another 10, 20, or 30 minutes." That suffering is unbearable for a child's mind. "What shall I do? Shall I kill the snake and let the frog out of the mouth of death, or shall I pass by and mind my own business?" In my child's mind it didn't give me satisfaction to run away from the scene.

Suppose I denied the snake its meal. Saving the frog's life would bring pain for the snake. I didn't know what to do, why such cruelty should exist. I asked several people, including my parents, for the answer but they couldn't give me one. Which is right? To kill the snake and let the frog go or just allow the frog to be eaten by the snake? Several days passed by. Every time I saw a frog in a snake I felt it very strongly in my heart. At last I decided I must evolve a philosophy of action. I decided to take a small stick and gently beat the snake until the frog was let free from the snake's mouth. I was sorry for the snake too, so I wouldn't kill the snake. Instead I would tell it, "When I am not here, you can catch a frog." That was how I solved my first philosophical problem, the problem of life and death. I don't know whether the snakes liked the solution or not, but that's the way it ended.

From then onwards a series of questions came into my mind. Though I was born in the Hindu religion, I couldn't accept everything without finding my own answers. I could not blindly follow all the rules and regulations. Though my parents were very religious, my understanding of religion was just like any other teenager's. To many of us what had been told by parents didn't make any sense. When I was in high school we had problems with the untouchables (the lowest group in the Hindu caste system). We could not play with the untouchable children or even go near them. If we went near we had to take baths, for purification, or we would not get admission into our home. Since the incident with the frog, many injustices—untouchability, suffering, hunger, death—all created a stir in my mind.

At the age of sixteen, having completed high school, Swamy Kuttan left his village for the first time and joined the army. This was during World War II, when recruiting standards were somewhat lax, allowing him to join even though he was under age. He had excelled in scientific subjects in high school and so was accepted as a recruit in the engineering corp. He left home partly because like any teenager he wanted to see the world, but also because he felt that something was pulling him. He completed basic training and was then stationed in Jalandhur in Northern India. His mind was still full of philosophical questions. He describes how he came to find the answers he needed.

One evening I had an argument with some of my friends, a silly argument, but it stirred up my whole mind: What is life? What is it? We keep doing the same things. We get up in the morning, we eat, we wash ourselves, we go to the office, we work, we give some orders, we take some orders, we make some money, we go to sleep, we enjoy. Is there anything beyond that? I decided to get away from all things and withdrew myself except for my official duties. The next morning I was looking for a lost letter in my office, but I couldn't see it anywhere. Perhaps the letter I was looking for was in the wastepaper basket. I looked there, but I didn't find the letter. I found something else.

In the wastepaper basket there was a divine message. It was a small leaflet which contained the essence of yoga. It was called

Sadhana Tattwa, or *Yoga Practices*. This was the first time I had ever seen anything like it. The man who wrote this leaflet, which was almost crumbling, was Sri Swami Sivananda of Rishikesh, Himalayas. I read the simple contents. With a few headlines it began, "An ounce of practice is better than tons of theories." Then he gave a simple way to find peace. He started with "Health Culture," then "Energy Culture," "Ethical Culture," "Will Culture," "Heart Culture," "Psychic Culture," and finally, "Spiritual Culture."

For Health Culture he asked us to do *asana* and *pranayama*. I didn't know anything about them, but I knew the meaning of the words. In Sanskrit, *asana* means "posture." In fact, I had seen it when I was a small child. A yogi came to my school and demonstrated the yoga postures, so I could remember that. At that time yoga itself was not that well known, so I wanted to study it. But I didn't just want to study yoga. All that was written in that pamphlet was what I was looking for. I felt I must find that man wherever he was. His writing actually pierced my heart.

To reach Rishikesh, Himalayas, about 600 to 700 miles from my army camp, was almost impossible during the war. In the first place one was not allowed to leave the camp for more than two hours a week, on Sunday. I wanted to go out of the camp for two or three days, which normally wasn't allowed. Anyhow, I made an application and waited to see what would happen. It was sanctioned; it was God's will.

I arrived in Rishikesh and saw Swami Sivananda for the first time. That meeting changed my whole idea of life. I expected to see Swami Sivananda sitting on a tiger skin, with a long beard, with flowers in his hand for blessing the students, the way one sees most of the swamis. I didn't believe in those religious hypocrites, but still I had that idea in my mind. To my astonishment, Swami Sivananda didn't have any tiger skin or flowers or students bowing before him. There was a group of pilgrims and visitors standing and sitting, asking him questions in a casual way. His answers were so beautiful and so precise and so simple.

I was among the crowd sitting far away. I could only stay for two minutes, that's all. I had to take a return bus or I'd be court-martialed. But those two minutes were worthwhile for me, to see him and know what type of person he is. I couldn't even come near him because I was very small and ignorant. What question could I ask him? There were hundreds of people there who were very intelligent, very educated, and spiritually evolved. I was a small young boy of seventeen; what kind of question could I ask

Swami Sivananda, Guru of Swami Vishnu-devananda

such a spiritual giant? But that was not important to me; when I looked at him I was satisfied. I saw for the first time a person who was sincere, and what he said was something direct, and when he smiled it was as if some energy were pouring from his face to mine. It touched my body and my mind; my whole body was in a kind ecstasy just looking at him. I left my future Master.

When you come in contact with a great soul, a saint, the most strange and marvelous things can happen. You sense a shift in your mind and spirit, a movement, an uplifting. Something has changed for the better. Sometimes these changes are obvious and dramatic: feelings of ecstasy, a strong sense of having known the person before, or even confusion, not knowing what's happened but sensing that an irrevocable change has taken place. The effects can also be more subtle. You may not even notice them at first, or at all. But on some level the contact has left a deep impression that will manifest when you are ready to deal with it.

Many people were deeply moved when they first met Swami Vishnu-devananda. Some of his students speak of their first meetings:

I was living in Crystal Lake, Illinois, in March of 1966, when a friend mentioned that an Indian monk was to give a demonstration of yoga at a Chicago hall the next day. Out of sheer curiosity my wife and I decided to go listen to the monk and observe the demonstration. Coming as I do from India, I was somewhat familiar with certain aspects of this spiritual discipline. But I had never seen an authentic performance of the physical aspects of yoga.

That afternoon Swami Vishnu-devananda spoke at some length on raja yoga as propounded by the Indian Sage, Patanjali. He took the audience through its eight limbs: *yama, niyama, asana, pranayama, pratyahara, dharana, dhyana*, and *samadhi*. In particular, he spoke of *asana* and *pranayama*, the aspects of raja yoga that have come to be known as hatha yoga. He referred to his book, *The Complete Illustrated Book of Yoga* and emphasized the virtues of vegetarianism.

The swami demonstrated several postures beginning with the headstand and then the shoulder stand, the plow, forward bends, and the balancing postures of crow and warrior. He concluded the forty-minute demonstration by displaying some *bandhas* (locks) and two breathing exercises. The audience listened with rapt attention and watched in pin-drop silence. The swami invited comments and questions, and I recall a heavyset gentleman asking with some audacity in his voice, "Where do you get your strength-giving proteins if you eat a vegetarian diet all the time?" The swami invited the questioner to test his strength while he demonstrated the bridge pose (a back arch with shoulders and feet on the floor and hips high in the air supported by the arms). He asked the gentleman to sit on his stomach. The man did not take the challenge and the episode ended in a roar of laughter.

Dr. Jagdish C. Prabhakar
Northridge, CA

ॐ नमो नारायणाय

I was very excited when I was about to meet Swami Vishnu for the first time. It was in Brur-Hail, Israel, two years after I took my teacher training. I had heard many stories about Swamiji. The room was packed with yoga students and followers sitting in candlelight. Swami Vishnu walked up to the podium, and with great intent prostrated to the picture of his *guru*, Swami Sivananda. In a split second I realized that this man dedicated his life to his teacher and his teachings. I experienced a deep sensation of love, and tears came to my eyes.

Ananda
Israel

ॐ नमो नारायणाय

The first time I met Swamiji was in San Francisco. A year before, a swami in Rishikesh, India told me about him. I was looking for a teacher in India, and he told me to go to Canada and see the "Flying Swami." But I was led to San Francisco.

Someone on the street there gave me a leaflet which said, "The Flying Swami is coming to town, lecture and *satsang* at 8:00 PM." I remembered the recommendation from Rishikesh and went to the lecture. The center was full of people. Swamiji gave a lecture and during the whole time he was speaking there was a man standing on his head. My mind was going through many thoughts, "stupid, brave, disturbing, ego. . ." I didn't think it was appropriate for him to do this during the lecture.

At the end of the program I pushed forward to be closer to Swamiji. I saw the headstand man next to him. Swamiji welcomed him with affection and told everybody who he was. He had just come out of the prison near San Francisco where, during a visit, Swamiji had left his Complete Illustrated Book of Yoga in the library. It changed the man's life, and out of thankfulness and appreciation he stood on his head during the lecture time to show Swamiji that he had learned something.

Swami Durgananda

ॐ नमो नारायणाय

I was 17 years old when I first met Swamiji. It was the spring of 1971. Our teacher had invited her students to join her in a weekend visit to the Val Morin *ashram*. High heeled shoes were in style that year and I left mine at the door to the Krishna Temple. There were no more than 15 people seated around Swamiji that day. I thought he was looking straight at me when he said, "If God would have wanted us to wear high heeled shoes, don't you think he would have put a bone sticking out of the foot?" I laughed with everyone else. There was no malice in his voice, just a simple statement of fact. I laugh now to hear his voice in my mind. Nothing has ever sounded truer to me.

I heard kirtan (spiritual songs) for the first time that weekend. When I left Val Morin on Sunday, I took with me a gift that has sustained me throughout the twenty years that followed, "Om Namo Bhagavate Vasudevaya." That mantra has vibrated in my heart and mind since the day I first heard it.

Radha
Montreal, Quebec, Canada

ॐ नमो नारायणाय

I first came to the yoga retreat in Nassau in 1976, for the April Yoga and Psychic Conference. My first sight of Swamiji was a surprise, for here was this large, earthy man with a warm, laughing face, beaming, walking around the retreat, unattended by flunkies, greeting people, seeing that things were going well.

Later, at the evening talent show, a young English, Monte Python-type comic sang a song to the tune of Belafonte's *Banana Boat Man.* "Swami Vishnu, he keep you happy all the time," was the refrain, and the litany was full of satirical references to the huge crowds at the retreat, the rows of people sleeping on the floor, the water going off, the lack of bathrooms, and so forth.

I looked over at Swami Vishnu, expecting to see anger, but instead saw him laughing even more heartily than before. This was a *guru* who did not expect one to worship him in hushed tones. Life was permitted, happiness was OK too, and humor was honored.

Silvia Goldsmith
New York City

ॐ नमो नारायणाय

I went to the Sivananda Yoga Vedanta Center in Tel Aviv, Israel, after my mother gave me a small advertisement which she had cut out from a newspaper. It was a listing for yoga classes, in which I was very interested. I didn't really like the look of the classified commercial ad, however, because I was quite busy looking for a way to get to India to find a great yogi in a cave who would liberate me from the trammels of my mind.

Immediately upon entering the center and being greeted by the young director, SivaDass, I had a strange feeling that I was "home" and some weight had been lifted from my shoulders. Since I had no money, SivaDass said he would teach me if I would clean the center daily. We began right away, me to clean, and he to go on and on about someone named Swamiji, who from his pictures seemed to be a chubby, cheery Indian man but didn't look at all like the cave *guru* I was looking for. SivaDass taught me *asanas* and meditation but mostly carried on extolling the virtues of his *guru,* this man called Swamiji.

Rukmini, the other staff member, would also join in, and whenever they recalled some story or other about Swamiji, their eyes seemed to sparkle with a special light.

This made me more curious to meet the man. Who was he and why did he make their eyes twinkle like that when they thought of him? Time went on, SivaDass and Rukmini had to return to the United States, and that man called Swamiji sent a middle-aged woman, Swami Dayananda, to direct the center. She was quite strict but seemed to me to know a lot about spiritual matters. She also went on and on about this Swamiji of hers and her eyes would likewise twinkle.

One day we learned that Swamiji was coming to visit for a few days. He would hold a retreat near Jerusalem as well as some programs in Tel Aviv. This news led to unbelievable excitement. Lots of things had to be suddenly arranged: people called, the center scrubbed and spruced, everything put in order, the retreat planned, halls hired for public talks, and ads placed.

A close friend of the center, Rachel Salzburg, offered to host Swamiji upon his arrival; her friends would prepare a special meal. There was lots of preparation and more bustling. To tell the truth I thought that all this work for a mere human was a little much, but my curiosity was definitely growing around the person who could cause such a hustle and bustle and so much obvious joy.

On the evening of Swamiji's arrival, Swami Dayananda and Rachel went to the airport, while about twenty-five people gathered at Rachel's apartment. We sat around chit-chatting and those who knew Swamiji told amusing anecdotes about him. But the plane was late and we got more and more restless and distracted. Some people had to leave.

Suddenly, after more than four hours of waiting, there was a tremendous bustle in the stairwell. Some force was heading up the four flights and was obviously coming our way. The door burst open with a rush of swirling energy and a very small Indian man in a brown raincoat and brown pants was standing right in front of me, looking up at me very intently.

My heart stopped when he reached out with both of his soft hands, grasped mine in them and said, "I've heard all about you." At that moment I felt that he was feeling my past, present and future through his hands and everything was known to him. The next second he was off around the room greeting old friends, laughing uproariously, meeting someone new, giving instructions to his secretary and Swami Dayananda. The odd thing was that now he seemed to be very tall and not short at all. I was confounded, shocked, dumbfounded and amazed all at once. He knew everything about me—my whole heart that I had kept hidden, he knew it just like that.

We all sat down around a big table to eat. The next shock. I had been brought up in a British Colonial manner, and even to have one's elbows on the dinner table was sacrilege. Now here was this swami mixing his food together on his plate with his hand! He was even squeezing the food through his fingers and putting it in his mouth with his hand, eating like mad, like a baby kid. He was also telling Rachel, who was busy piling food up on his plate, that he was a "good boy. Look, I'm eating everything." I could hardly comprehend this near barbaric scene and my mind began to short circuit. I stared open mouthed. Swamiji returned the stare and, in the middle of a conversation with someone else, asked me my age. I just managed to stammer it out but he was already talking to someone else.

He picked up a jug of water, held it up at arm's length, tilted his head back, and poured half the contents straight down his throat from about a foot above his head. This was too much for me. "No manners at all," I thought. (Only later when I came to India and saw everyone eating and drinking in that same way did I realize that this was a cultural norm.)

That night as I lay awake my whole being was filled with the extraordinary presence of this person, who was at once so small and big, so near and far, so caring, perceptive, and seemingly not bothered about what others thought of his ways. He was indeed quite a mysterious person. As I fell asleep I think my eyes were twinkling a little, just thinking about him.

Swami Sankarananda

ॐ

Finding the *Guru*

What is a *guru*? Literally *gu* means "darkness" and *ru* means "light." A *guru* leads one from darkness to light. A *guru* is a man or woman spiritual teacher who leads their students to God-realization. They can be famous men and women, like Mahatma Ghandi or Anandamayi Ma, or someone who is known by only one student. A *guru* is not an ordinary teacher; he or she is a God-realized soul or on the path towards universal consciousness. The *guru* imparts spiritual knowledge to the student, pointing the way towards the truth, but the student achieves liberation through his or her own effort.

Swami Sivananda, the *guru* of Swami Vishnu-devananda, gives the following definition of *guru* in his book Bliss Divine.

> "The *sadguru* is Brahman (God) himself. He is an ocean of bliss, knowledge, and mercy. He is the captain of your soul. He is a fountain of joy. He removes all your troubles, sorrows and obstacles. He shows you the right divine path. He tears your veil of ignorance. He makes you immortal and divine. He transmutes your lower diabolical nature. He gives you the rope of knowledge, and takes you up when you are drowning in this ocean of samsara. Do not consider him to be only a man. If you take him as a man, you are a beast. Worship your *guru* and bow to him with reverence."

Swami Vishnu-devananda gave the following description of how he came to realize that Sivananda was his *guru*:

> When I got my army leave, even before I thought of going home, (about 2000 miles south), I decided to go to Rishikesh and stay with Swami Sivananda in his *ashram* for two days. I wanted to learn from him and ask him some questions.
>
> It was almost evening when I arrived at the *ashram*. Swami Sivananda was leaving his tiny office with some disciples, going down the hill to the bank of the Ganges, where his cottage is situated. I was going towards the office and he was coming out of the office, so I would come face to face with him.
>
> Now I realized I had a problem. In India it is customary to bow our heads before all saints, all swamis, all holy people. Swami Sivananda was not only a swami and a holy man, he was also considered to be one of the greatest masters of India. But I was

not ready to bow my head to anyone. I would not bow to any holy man, including Swami Sivananda, because after all, all human beings are equal. Why should I bow my head to him or anyone else? But I thought if I stood in front of him without bowing my head, it would be a rude way of behaving towards anybody, especially a holy man. I didn't want to be rude to him, especially in front of his disciples. It was so awkward for me that I immediately left the path and hid myself in a corner, planning to let Sivananda and his disciples pass me by.

Sivananda continued coming down the path, and as he neared the place where I stood, he suddenly looked up and saw me hiding in the corner. He came straight towards me. "You have come from Jalandhur," he said, and he bowed before me and touched my feet!

I stood there like a statue. This great man, a giant actually, (of course he is a spiritual giant, but also physically he was quite tall, over 6 feet) bowed before a silly idiot stupid me, touching my feet. That touch, that action, shook my whole body. And that was the first time I ever bowed my head to another person. I fell at the feet of Swami Sivananda at that moment, with all my heart, with all my love. Until that day I did not think that any human being on this earth could make me bow my head, especially with such love and devotion.

Swami Sivananda taught me in this simple way. He saw what was hidden in my heart; he saw my dirt, my egoistic nature, and without hesitation he taught me great humility.

The higher you go into the spiritual heights the humbler you will be, and Sivananda proved that to a simple boy like me. At that moment I accepted him as my teacher, my Master, my everything. Swami Sivananda then asked me to stay for a couple of days. I answered, "Yes, I will stay." Then he asked one of his disciples to take me to the kitchen and get me something to eat.

On that same first evening, just at sunset, all Sivananda's disciples assembled in front of the Ganges to worship the river. Naturally, for me it was superstitious to worship a flowing river. Was there any meaning in it? I thought that all of Swami Sivananda's disciples must be illiterate fools. They didn't know anything about water or rivers. Water is made up of H_2O. I was a little scientific minded in my childhood; in school I learned chemistry, physiology, electronics, and so forth. Not only that, but in my chemistry class I myself made water out of hydrogen and oxygen. None of the disciples at Sivananda *Ashram* seemed to know anything about that. They were worshipping the silly Ganges!

Anyhow, it was a beautiful scene because of the sunset and the majestic Himalayas in the background and the flowing river. On either side the swamis in orange robes were sitting and meditating, chanting and bell ringing. It was very beautiful, no doubt about it, but for me worshipping the Ganges was just superstition. "It's just a river; what is this?" I thought as I watched the whole ceremony.

Then Swami Sivananda came and joined his disciples. I couldn't understand that because even though the disciples might be illiterate, Sivananda was not. Before he became a swami he was a medical doctor. "A medical doctor who doesn't know this much, that water is made up of H_2O, what kind of doctor is he?" As I was thinking like that about Sivananda, he came to join the group. At the very moment that I thought, "How can a doctor not know anything about H_2O?" Sivananda turned his head towards me gently—he said nothing—and then turned back again to join the worship of the Ganges.

Suddenly I saw no more Ganges; the river disappeared. In its place I saw a mass of light flowing with the message, "Everything is God, even this flowing river is God. Do not use your tiny intellect to understand God, the Infinite. Your intellect is finite; your understanding of chemistry, physiology, science, biology, physics, mathematics is nothing; your knowledge is so little, so finite, so tiny that you have not even touched one grain of sand on the vast beach. Far beyond your intellect, far beyond your understanding, lies inexhaustible knowledge and wealth, strength and power, peace and joy. Do not use your intellect to find the answers for God and his manifestations. Everything is God."

I learned two very difficult lessons on the same day. The first lesson taught me humility, because I thought I was very great. The second lesson taught me that I didn't know anything about anything. So I had two hard lessons that day. There was no more doubting Sivananda. That day was sufficient.

After a two-day stay, Swamiji went to visit his family in Kerala and then returned to the army camp to complete his tour of duty. During this time he started practicing *asanas* and *pranayama* and meditating, learning from books he bought at the *ashram*. After he left the army he went home briefly but was drawn back to Rishikesh and Sivananda. He returned for another "brief visit" but ended up staying for ten years.

At this point in his narrative he was twenty years old.

Swami Sivananda passed by; he was leaving his office work. He looked at me and said, "Hmm, stay here."

"Yes Swamiji." That was all I said without even thinking. Then I understood. Why did I give my word, that I would stay? According to the early training in my home with my parents, if you say you are going to do something, if you give your word, you cannot take it back under any conditions. Now I had given my word not to an ordinary person, but to a great sage. I said I would stay. It was so clear and now here I was, I was stuck. I could not go back home; I gave my word. So I settled in the Sivananda *Ashram* with my Master's blessings, not knowing whether I really had the strength to take my new life. But there was some type of peace and joy in knowing that my future would be under the guidance of a great master.

There was also a type of false satisfaction in what I did. I was pleased that I might be able to know more about *kundalini*, in which I had great interest. I wanted to learn hatha yoga, *kundalini* yoga, and so on. So I thought, "Master must have seen something in me, some greatness." I thought he was going to initiate me into *kundalini* yoga and I would be able to raise my *kundalini*. "That's why I've been practicing yoga for more than a year and a half now; I think now I must be ready for such a deep initiation." With this false notion I accepted his request and stayed at the *ashram*, not knowing Master's real intention.

The next morning, to my amazement, Master asked me to go to the guests' rooms to pick up their soiled clothes and wash them in the river. I had been given the job of cleaning the clothes of the guests! I could not comprehend why Master should give me that type of work. You may not be able to understand it, because you've been born into a different type of society, but when you are born in India, in an upper-class caste, you are told not to do any type of menial work. Since childhood you would have been told this. It's put into your brain; you can't break out so easily. I thought, "What is the use of all this washing clothes? I came to learn yoga; I came to awaken *kundalini;* I came to see God!"

But Master had his own way of training. Each individual who came to the Master had a specific type of fault. He saw from the very beginning, from our first meeting, that my whole problem was ego. It was extreme; I was egoistic and I still am to a certain extent. So if I was going to go anywhere near to God-realization, I had to break this. From the very beginning Master's training was to break this greatest fault in me, my greatest dirt, the ego. So he gave me the most difficult job of all to do. It was not the energy; that's really nothing. It didn't take more than half an hour's work to wash a half dozen clothes. That was not it; it was the suffering I was undergoing. For me to do such a job was very painful, far beyond your understanding.

From these early lessons comes the core of Swamiji's teaching: see God in everything and everyone, and serve them with humility. If you sincerely practice this simple teaching, slowly your ego will shrink and your heart will grow.

How do you know when you have found your *guru*? Unfortunately this is like asking the proverbial question, How many angels can dance on the head of a pin? Some people just know, almost instantaneously, intuitively, when they come in contact with their teacher. Others struggle for years, doubting, questioning, wondering, hoping. There is no easy answer. All that can be said is that when you know, you know.

> I wish I could say that I had the instant reverence for Swamiji that he had for Sivananda, but I would not be telling the truth. He sort of grew on me slowly. I saw him first in 1978 at the *ashram* in Val Morin during the busy summer season. I'd gone to spend the weekend and "check out the scene." During morning and evening *satsang* Swamiji would sit up at the front of the yoga hall and talk. What he said was interesting, often entertaining, and always applied to spiritual life. But he was this funny little Indian guy! I respected him for his knowledge, but I certainly didn't feel any reverence.
>
> I kept going back to the *ashram*. I liked the sense of community, I liked the classes, I liked all the people I met there. My personal relationship with Swamiji started out when I met him on the path one day. I didn't have anything to say to him, but out of respect I bowed. He smiled and bowed back. That was our entire relationship for the next while, bowing and smiling at each other. He gradually found out my name, and would sometimes say a few words, but I kept my distance, even as I became more involved in the *ashram* and the organization, teaching classes and telling everyone I could about this wonderful place in the Laurentians.
>
> One day, when I was having great emotional difficulties, I asked if I could speak to Swamiji privately, hoping for some advice that could calm my mind and show me the way out of my predicament. I told him what my problems were while he listened and smiled. I could really feel his love for me, and his sympathy for my problems. He advised me on what to do, and how what he said fit with a yogic life. I felt a new closeness with Swamiji, a new sense of a personal relationship with him. But still I couldn't completely surrender. I held back. It was fine to ask for his advice, but I wouldn't let him direct my life as I saw others around me do. I knew what was best for me.
>
> In the summer of 1986 Swamiji started planning a tour of India for the following year, to commemorate the 100th anniversary of Sivananda's birth. He was inviting students to go with him. My wife and I discussed it and decided she would go while I stayed home to take care of our two children. They were then seven and twelve years old. It just seemed too impractical to leave them with friends and relatives while we both went off to India for six weeks.
>
> Several times through the summer and fall Swamiji would ask me if I was going to India with him. Every time I'd tell him, "No Swamiji, Madalasa is going but I have to stay home and take care of the children." He would seem to accept my answer, but the next time he'd see me he'd ask the same question again. I got fairly frustrated with him. I thought, "These *sanyasins* have no

understanding of family life." He was incredibly persistent, and I was stubbornly resistant. At the same time I was feeling kind of guilty. If he was my teacher, why wasn't I paying attention to him, doing what he said. My practical mind said one thing, my heart said another.

At New Years I went to the *ashram* for two days, deciding that if Swamiji asked me one more time to go to India I would just have to give in. Over the two days I saw him several times but it was like I wasn't even there. He didn't greet me, or talk to me, or even mention my name in passing. This was most unusual and upsetting for me. What had happened to my personal relationship with him? Finally it was one o'clock in the morning New Years Eve. The special programs were over and Swamiji was getting ready to leave. I was going home in the morning, and wouldn't see him again for a long time. I was standing at the back of a crowd of fifty or sixty people, feeling depressed and thinking, "Oh well, I guess I'm not going to India."

Just then, Swamiji turned and looked at me and said "Gopala Krishna, go to India."

I answered, "Yes Swamiji." He turned away and didn't say another word.

I was totally amazed. How did he know what I was thinking? How did he know at that precise moment that I was ripe to finally let go and say yes, to just accept him? I felt a great wave of relief and elation. I wasn't at all worried about how it would work out; I just knew it would be O.K. Swamiji would make sure of it.

Gopala Krishna

ॐ नमो नारायणाय

It took me years to accept Swami Vishnu as my *guru.* Somehow he just didn't fit my image of a *guru* early on.

My first yoga teacher in Fredericton, New Brunswick, had studied with Swamiji and the Montreal centre in the early 1960's. Swamiji used to do asanas with the students there. I really enjoyed my Sivananda yoga classes. One evening my teacher brought a tape to class of kirtan with Swami Vishnu. I was excited by it, but wasn't sure what to make of it.

After I left Fredericton I was always searching for a good yoga class. I was living in Boston for a while, and attended the class closest to the Sivananda style I could find. I went to their *ashram* where I met their *guru,* Swami Satchidananda. Was I ever impressed! A straight, tall man, so stately. When I saw him enter the yoga hall I wondered if his feet were on the ground or whether he was floating over it. "Ah, a *guru,*" I was sure.

When I first saw Swami Vishnu at teacher training in Nassau in 1982, I couldn't believe it. He was shouting at staff, barking orders, plowing along. No quietude, no floating. He seemed angry. After teacher training, a six-month hitch to teach at the Montreal centre became a five and one-half year commitment in Montreal and Val Morin, all of it in close proximity to Swamiji. I was always unsure, a bit wary, wondering if he was, could be, my *guru.*

Sometimes I felt he must be. Working in the organization year after year, I was impressed by his laughter, his joy, the wisdom at *satsang*. Other times I was not so sure. The shouting, the sometimes strained relations with current and former students, disturbed me. After five years I couldn't even be certain that Swamiji would remember my name from week to week. Over the years my wariness of Swamiji wore down, but still I wasn't sure if he was my *guru*, my teacher, the remover of darkness.

The time finally came for me to leave the organization to start family life. I was a staff member at the *ashram* in Val Morin at the time. I was called to Swamiji's house with Michael, another staff member, for an accounting meeting. It was an extraordinary meeting.

Michael had some personal questions to ask Swamiji and received some personal advice. Then Swamiji turned to me and said, "Arjuna, now you are going out into the world. It won't be easy...", and continued to give me personal advice, marital advice, support. I was amazed: he knew me, he knew me deeply, and my wife too. He said, "Arjuna, you don't know it, but I know all my students, love them, care for them deeply. I care what happens to them." I had never heard anything like this before, never heard Swamiji use that tone. At that moment I knew he was my *guru*. "Take your mantra with you and repeat it; you'll need it to protect you in the world," he said.

> Arjuna
> Aylmer, Quebec, Canada

ॐ नमो नारायणाय

I met Swamiji for the first time in January, 1987, at the end of the Teacher Training Course at Neyyar Dam, India. Everybody was looking forward to his visit. When he arrived, the atmosphere was filled of bhakti, everyone was repeating "Om Namo Narayanaya," prostrating at his feet and throwing flowers on the ground in front of him. I started weeping, first lightly, then more and more intensely. My emotions do not usually manifest externally and I found no apparent reason for it this time.

I have been reflecting a long time about this event and a few months ago got the feeling that Swamiji was a *guru* in previous lifetimes and was meeting some of his old disciples again. I do not like to speculate very much about past lives, but it seems the only acceptable explanation for me. When one meets a good friend or relative after a long time, one might cry just because of the intense emotion. This event was definitely something very important in my life. It is probably because of it that I decided to stop my search for another path or *guru*.

> Swami Atmaramananda

ॐ नमो नारायणाय

Swamiji often told us that he had been our *guru* in previous lifetimes. Instead of doing his duty to us in his previous lifetime, he had run away to meditate in the forest, leaving us to struggle on our own. He had to reincarnate and become our *guru* again to complete his obligation to us. Many people had this *deja vu* experience on first meeting him. Others came to accept Swamiji as their *guru* in other ways.

I first came to The Yoga Ranch in Woodbourne in the late fall of 1983 with my husband, Jim. We took classes and helped on weekends. We first met Swamiji briefly that winter, and then again after we'd joined the staff and were taking teacher training in the fall of 1984.

I was confused about the meaning of *guru* and the need for one. Although I felt very close to Swami Sivananda, I still had many doubts about who Swami Vishnu-devananda was. Then, after taking mantra initiation, I had a powerful dream: Swamiji came to me in the dream, dressed all in white and enveloped in a blazing light. He brought his face very close to mine, looked at me with a mischievous smile, and said, "I am your *guru* you know."

I replied, "I know Swamiji, but you are so different and strange, I just don't understand."

But Swamiji looked deeply at me and my doubts vanished. I somehow understood inside myself that even though he was beyond anything I could ever understand, Swamiji was my *guru*.

After that I often dreamt of Swamiji. Once I was troubled about getting a spiritual name. Jim felt very strongly that he didn't want me to change my name to a Sanskrit one. Swamiji came in a dream and said, "Don't worry about getting a name. It doesn't matter. Let it be as it is."

These dreams were not like regular dreams. I felt they were real visits from Swamiji. The feeling of peace and inspiration afterwards was the same as when being in his presence. Once when Swamiji came to the ranch I asked him if he knew about my dreams. He smiled knowingly and said, "Don't dream about Swami Vishnu, dream about Lord Vishnu."

Lisa
Woodbourne, NY, USA

ॐ नमो नारायणाय

Last month (December, 1984), I rode up to Canada with the staff of the New York Sivananda Center to spend Christmas and New Year's Eve with Swami Vishnu at the *ashram* in Val Morin. We first drove to the ranch in upstate New York, then traveled north through the Adirondacks, past Montreal, and on into the Laurentian Mountains. When we arrived in Val Morin it was snowing heavily. The staff members went down to Swamiji's house for a visit, but I didn't see him until *satsang* when he spoke about the Star of Bethlehem, and asked us to visualize it mentally. As he spoke my mind began to wander. I said to myself, "All this star talk is getting rather boring." Suddenly, as I sat there with my eyes closed, I saw a brilliant star-shaped form. I thought, "He may repeat himself, but it sure works." I marveled at the extraordinary effect of his mind on my consciousness.

I continued, nevertheless, to find fault with him during my entire stay. When he arrived for meditation, I'd wonder, "Who is making all that noise?" A heavy-footed, out-of-breath person had come into the room, with a great deal of undignified huffing and puffing. I'd peek, and there Swamiji would be, wearing a rather grumpy expression on his face, and tucking his feet under him as he settled into his massive, orange-upholstered chair. He'd cough, too, which I found distracting.

Was this the holy man I'd so revered in New York in the fall, when he performed puja in honor of Devi, the great Goddess? I'd been so overwhelmed by Swami Vishnu's holiness then, that I'd begged him to initiate me into a mantra on the spot. Ever since I'd been faithfully repeating my mantra and trying hard to meditate. But I was getting nowhere. I'd gone to Val Morin hoping that Swamiji would help me break through my meditation gridlock. Now that I was finally in his presence, I didn't quite know what to make of him.

The day after Christmas it sleeted for hours, and Swamiji was trapped in his house by the ice, because the road leading up the steep hill from his house was too difficult for him to maneuver. At first it was announced that there would be no meditation. Then we were told that it would be held but without Swamiji. I think we all felt disconsolate at this prospect; I certainly did. I longed to spend as much time with him as possible even though he puzzled me, or maybe because of it. So I was thrilled when we were invited to come to his house to meditate.

Twenty of us trooped down the icy road to Swamiji's residence and were seated in the adjoining greenhouse. A big whirlpool bath filled with steaming water was at one end of the room; hanging plants were dripping condensation on our heads. The humid, lush atmosphere was a welcome contrast to the icy world outside, but it wasn't the ascetic, Spartan environment I'd expected. A late arrival, I sat in the only place left, right at the foot of Swamiji's orange chair. I looked around nervously and wondered how I was supposed to act.

At last he arrived. He took some time to settle into his chair and then informed us that he wasn't going to talk. Rather, he was going to lead us in meditation. Succinctly and beautifully he explained mediation and mantras, and then entered the meditative state. I could see that because I wasn't meditating; I was peeking at him. I pulled myself together and began to labor mightily to still my mind. No dice. I was so disappointed. Surely sitting this close to Swamiji, right smack dab in his energy field, I would begin to make some progress. "Please, Guru, purify my mind," I prayed, and I meant it. Nothing. I resigned myself to simply basking in his aura and accepted this as all I was ready for. Then he scratched himself. "How's this?" I thought. "Can even he fidget and scratch?" But the thought soon fled my mind, for no sooner did he scratch himself than for the first time, I entered a blissful mental state.

After the meditation period ended, Swamiji led us in chanting Om Namo Narayanaya for fifteen minutes. He dismissed us then saying, "That Mantra will help you purify the mind." I thought he looked at me directly, and gave me a little business-like nod.

The day we were to leave, it was snowing heavily. Swamiji called all us New Yorkers down to the house to say good-bye. He greeted us sitting by his desk in a black leather swivel chair, his feet tucked under him. We sat on the floor and drank hot chocolate. At Swamiji's request, someone read out loud some promotional material about building a computer from scratch with a kind of Heath-kit. We couldn't help giggling at the obviously exaggerated promises of the promotional material, but Swamiji insisted on hearing the whole thing. He was all excited about the idea of making a computer on his own, with the aid of a young staff member. I hadn't exactly envisioned my *guru* as being a Popular Mechanics buff, but I had to admit that I liked his capacity for boyish excitement. Certainly he had an inquiring mind.

I found that my eyes hurt when I looked at Swamiji, and that I was almost stupefied by the power of his presence. The fact that his attention was confined to only a few people seemed to intensify his energy. He chatted with us as we drank our chocolate, and I was gratified to see that he knew me a little by now. After all, Ambika and I had put on a play in honor of his birthday, on New Year's Eve. Since then, at meditation, I'd had the distinct impression that he was checking to see if I was there. Perhaps we all had that feeling?

He fed us Mozart balls and candies, and then dismissed us with his blessing. But the snow continued, and later in the afternoon we heard that Swamiji wouldn't allow us to leave in such a storm. We were to leave next morning at 5:30, when the snow was expected to let up.

Early the next morning we were outside, stomping through the snow to pack the car. It was pitch dark, and eerily silent. Suddenly Swamiji appeared with a flashlight walking up from his house on his way to mediation. He cut an amazing figure in his orange robe, army boots, beat-up orange down jacket and orange turban. He greeted us warmly and then fervently prayed for our safety. He blessed each of us and went on his way, turning back once or twice to bless us some more. I have a distinct mind picture of Swami Vishnu in his amazing attire, standing in the snow, with the dark all around us, absolutely radiating love and concern.

We piled into the car and drove off. The roads were atrocious and we skidded dangerously several times. I was awfully glad of Swamiji's blessing. After Montreal the highway condition improved, and we settled in for the long trip back to New York. I stared out the window and mentally reviewed my recent encounters with Swamiji. I couldn't understand him. He was obviously so holy, and at the same time, obviously such a character. "At least he wasn't putting on airs," I thought. No, he presented himself as a person, just like me. In any case, I decided, I wasn't fooled by his lack of pretension. I knew him for what he was: adorable Gurudev.

Saraswati
New York City

With the Master

Swamiji spent most of the years from 1947 to 1957 at Sivananda's *ashram* in Rishikesh, learning from and serving one of India's greatest contemporary saints. It was not always easy to stay. He had left his family home, 2000 miles to the south. Being the only son, his family expected him to return. Where did his duty lie, with his family or with his *guru*? He struggled with this problem. In his words:

After about six months' stay there was a tug of war in my mind. When you come for the first time to the *ashram*, or to a master, you think it will be much easier for you; everything is new. It is something like coming from a hot desert. Suddenly you come under a shady tree, cool with a lot of water, and how does it feel? So marvelous, is it not? Oh, you take the water, you splash in it, you sit under the cool shade. But if you are staying every day at the same pool, under the same tree, how does it feel after some time? It becomes monotonous. But the first time you come, it's so wonderful.

It's the same thing when you go to an *ashram* or a master. When you first arrive, you are coming from the world where it is just like a desert; the people are all negative, thoughts are negative, everyone is trying to cut everyone else's throat. But when you come to the *ashram*, everything is pure, the people are all good, and everyone is trying to help others. They are not perfect yet, but though each has his own faults, he wants to correct them. There are a lot of problems in *ashrams*; they are not actually as holy as you think. You find from saints to sinners there, and sometimes in the guise of spiritual aspirants, rogues come in to get away from the police. So it is very difficult in the *ashram*; there is every type of temperament and condition. But still, being under the master is like being under a huge tree. Everyone can sit under that tree and enjoy the shade. There is no partiality in this tree; its shade is completely open to anyone who comes under it. We are just the scorched people coming from the towns and villages and various parts of the world and the master is like a huge tree giving shade to everyone who comes.

After some time, even in this shade, your mind slowly starts feeling the monotony. So the terrible trouble then came to me: one portion of my mind began pulling me back to my home, to the old *samskaras*, you know, my father, mother, home, family, sisters. The other side of my mind was pulling me to stay with the Master because I gave my word. Which way to go? Shall I go and serve my parents and stay with them or shall I stay with my Master? I couldn't live with this mind; I couldn't take any more! So I approached my Master saying, "What shall I do?"

I wasn't strong enough to go directly and tell him my problems because we always gave respect to our Master and I was very close to him. It was very difficult for me to approach asking such a question. This much I knew, that my heart was pulling me towards my parents. So I wrote a small note explaining my state of mind.

My parents loved me; they had written several letters by this time and were expecting me. They never knew that I wanted to stay at the *ashram,* but now, after six months, they surmised as much. They wrote telling me to come back home and live with them, look after my father's land and take charge of my responsibilities, as they were getting old. This is our way; these are the customs in India. One takes care of one's parents, especially if one is male. It is his duty to take care of them, and so they expected me to be home.

But I also had other obligations. I had given my word to my Master and I also felt strong love towards him, towards his organization and his mission. So I wrote, "My parents are pulling in one direction, I want to go back home. I also want to stay here and serve. I don't know which way to go. I have terrible agony now in my heart; I want your advice. What shall I do? Shall I go back home or shall I stay?"

What was Sivananda's answer? *"Mata nasti, Peeta nasti."* It means, "for you, neither mother nor father." This is a great philosophical formula. In innumerable past lives I had mothers and fathers. In this life also there was a father and mother, but they are not going to be here eternally. That was all he said; he didn't say much. But that was sufficient, because I knew what he meant. He could see everything that was happening in me and in my future. At that time I was still young; I couldn't understand, I didn't know what he saw, I didn't even believe what he saw, but I accepted.

It seems very cruel to say to a young man to forget his father and mother. Master said if I had gone back home it's sure I would never be happy because I was not intended to live in that type of small family, with friends, a few children, and so on. That is not inherent in my mind at all; I could not see that at that time. Now,

I can see what state I would be in. There is no idea of individual family life; it's not there.

After that day I never considered anymore that I had only one father and one mother, but now the other beings in this universe are all my father and mother. That is the teaching I learned from my great Master. I was a little bit more peaceful and strong, then definitely ready to stay. Still, I had to go through several stages. So many things I had to pass through; this was only the first beginning stage of my life.

What did Sivananda really mean when he told Swamiji "You have no mother or father?" Sivananda was a medical doctor. He knew that physically Swamiji had to have had a father and mother, but he was speaking in a higher sense, using this opportunity to teach a greater truth. As long as we think we are this body, as long as we identify with father, mother, family, our physical reality, we cannot understand our true nature. In our essence, our soul, we are one with God, not separate or individualized. Our true nature is beyond the body, and in that sense we have no one father and mother. We are both birthless and deathless.

Soon after this incident Swamiji took vows of *brahmacharya*, giving up the pleasures of the senses, and taking the name Vishnu Chaitanya. Then in March of 1948 he took his *sanyas* vows, becoming Swami Vishnu-devananda.

The new Swami Vishnu-devananda became Sivananda's personal assistant, spending most of every day with him, and being with Sivananda every moment that he spent in public. In close daily contact with such a great saint, he learned many lessons very quickly. It is different from being with a normal teacher, someone who teaches you mathematics, or auto repair, or some other skill. Here's how Swamiji explained it.

It's not that we implicitly and blindly follow any teacher, but once we have accepted the teacher as our own, we know that the teacher's intention is only to help us, to show us the right path. We understand that the teacher can see our heart, and what portion he first has to try to correct before he can open the light. Your mind is just like a mirror. If there is some dirt on the mirror it is all cloudy and you can't see your image clearly. Is there any use then in just cleaning your face? If you want to see the image, you first have to clean the mirror.

Your mind is a mirror which has been completely clouded by lust, anger, greed, hatred, jealousy, envy, fear, selfishness, egoism, and a superiority complex if, like me, you come from a high caste family. As long as this dirt exists you can't see your image clearly. So from the very beginning of my training Master helped me see more clearly. Later on I understood why, but not in the beginning. I look back now and I can see the whole situation, how systematically, step by step, without even telling me, without mentioning anything, he tried to remove some of my impurities.

Swamiji receiving initiation from Swami Sivananda. The traditional method involves tracing the Sanskrit mantra in a bowl of sand.

They were very much at home with me. It is like some spot on
your clothes which you cannot just wash out with ordinary
detergent; you have to use special enzymes which may even eat
the clothing itself. In the same way he had to use some special
type of enzyme, to break up this type of dirt in my heart.

Sivananda taught mainly by example. Being a living example of oneness with
God, he encouraged others to be the same. What Swamiji taught, and even how he
taught it, comes directly from Sivananda. This is the greatness of the Indian
tradition. Each teacher passes on what he knows to his students, who in turn pass
it on to their own students in one continuous, unending stream of wisdom.
Swamiji was constantly observing a living saint in action and he learned many
lessons from what he saw.

Master always carried three ordinary cloth bags. One contained
the important correspondence which he would give to the various
swamis in charge of various departments. Another contained his
personal things: fountain pens, glasses, and so forth. The third
one contained fruits, nuts, and snacks. You may wonder why. It
wasn't for him.

One of his mottoes is "Serve, Love, Give, Purify, Meditate,
Realize." That's the basic motto of Swami Sivananda, his basic
philosophy. Serve and love and give. Without giving you can't
serve and love, you know. If you keep everything for yourself and
say, "O yes, I love you all," and if you eat without giving
something to others, that's not loving. You have to show your love
in action. So Master served and loved. He shared everything,
everything; he never kept anything. If there were two fruits, he
would immediately give one to others and then he'd eat part of
the other one.

In like manner, Swami Vishnu-devananda shared his food. You could never visit
him without him feeding you. Before you ever got a chance to say anything, he
would make sure you had something to eat and drink. Even if you just came to the
house to fix a broken tap or do some other maintenance chore, with no thought of
even seeing him, there was no escape.

I took the Yoga Teachers Training in 1979. One day early in my visit I was
asked to go to Swamiji's house to do some karma yoga (selfless service) in the
yard. I remember how determined I was to do a good job. When I arrived I
stood for a minute looking at the Sivalingam in the middle of the lagoon.
Swamiji came out of his house and, because he was practicing mouna (silence)
that Summer, motioned for me to take the chainsaw and to complete a
removal of a rather large stump from the ground. I'm 5'6", 120 lbs. and the
stump looked like a big tough bull moose that would not budge. I smiled,
nodded, grabbed the saw and started pulling on the starter chord. Away I went,

attacking that stump as though my very life depended on it.

When I was about half way through, the saw stopped. I grabbed the starter chord and started pulling and pulling and pulling. After a couple of minutes I felt a tap on my shoulder. I turned around and there was Swamiji with a a note reading "Out of gas?" I opened up the gas cap and sure enough it was empty. I nodded, and he roared with laughter. I asked where there was more gas and he pointed back to the camp. So I ran, and I mean ran, back to camp and ran back again with the gas can and completed the job, whereupon Swamiji showered me with fresh fruit: peaches, nectarines, plums, grapes, bananas.

Balarama

Sivananda had a regular daily routine. His cottage was down by the Ganges, and his office was further up the hill. Twice daily he would walk up and down the hill, to and from the office. As Sivananda's personal assistant, Swamiji would always accompany him.

> I'd be carrying the bags as we walked from his *kutir* to the office, and the other devotees would be following. Master would walk in the front and on the way he would deliver tidbits. It was only about a fifteen minute walk and he didn't talk too much, but sometimes he would make the trip a little longer by stopping to tell a few anecdotes or ask a few questions about one's welfare or health. Maybe a new guest had come and he would say, "How are you? Where do you come from? Do you keep a spiritual diary?" Then he would ask after their spiritual welfare and their family affairs. He was happy to encourage and help in any way people wanted him to. Each of the devotees thought that Sivananda took special care of him.
>
> That's the beauty of a great master. Everyone thought that Sivananda loved him more than anyone else; I also feel Sivananda loved me more than anyone else. All of the devotees thought the same thing. "Sivananda loves me more than anyone else." I actually think that only one other person had this quality: Lord Krishna. When he was in the physical world every *gopi* thought that Krishna loved her better that any other *gopi* because they reached oneness with him. In this way we were all happy to be near Master and to get this feeling, more and more every day.

Many lessons came from observing Sivananda in his day-to-day activities, but perhaps the strongest lesson came from something extraordinary that occurred. Swamiji told this story to us many times. He never seemed to tire of it, or the lesson it taught him.

> One morning Govinda, one of Master's new students, (he had been there only for six months), came to Master. He said he

wanted to go back home. So Master asked why.

"Oh, I don't know; I just have to go back."

Master knew this man's life. He was a married man in his early twenties and his wife had committed suicide because of him; she couldn't take life with him anymore. He had no peace of mind; he had absolutely lost himself. So he came to Sivananda's *ashram*. It was not his intention to stay there permanently, only to get some peace, maybe do a little work. So Master gave him some simple work and asked him to do *japa* (mantra repetition) for peace of mind. Master was very compassionate to people like this.

After six months, he wanted to go back home. Well, there's no harm if he wants to go back, but he also demanded the fare to go home. His home was in South India, 2,000 miles away, and our *ashram* was always in debt. Master gave away more than what came in; that was his nature. He fed about 200 people daily so we had to have food for them. Always there were debts, debts and debts. He also wrote and printed books and gave them away; free books, free literature, free food. It was because his heart was always wanting to give. So there was no money. Things were so bad in the early days that sometimes a few swamis had to go outside the *ashram* and beg for food. So Master said to Govinda that day, "It is not possible at present. We do not have the money. Stay for a few more months and get yourself peace of mind instead of going back home."

Govinda was not satisfied with that. He left Master and went to his room. The next evening after supper I was, as usual, carrying Master's bags. A few other people were coming along up to the Vedanta hall where we meditated in the evening. As we were going up Master asked me, "Vishnu Swami,"—that's the way he addressed me—"Where is Govinda's room?"

"Swamiji, I think he's staying at such and such a place."

"Take me there first, before we go to the Yoga Hall. Let us go there; I want to talk with him."

Master's mind must have been hurting since he refused Govinda, because he couldn't say no to anyone. That was his heart. But he didn't have any money. If he had, he'd have given it immediately. But he still had the feeling of the man, the hurt feeling. That's another motto of his, never hurt others' feelings. He knew he had hurt the feelings of another man, so he wanted at least to apologize. So he said, "Please take me there to him."

I led him. I used to have a lantern at night, a small hurricane lantern, and I was using it. In the dim light we were walking up the mountain to various cottages to find the room. Other devotees were following in their general way. Master knocked on the door and Govinda opened. He was in a very depressed mood. Master said, "Govinda, how are you?"

He didn't answer.

"You really want to go home? You're not just not feeling well? You really want to go home?"

Govinda just shrugged, but never answered anything, yes or no. Perhaps because he was hot, perhaps because he was angry. We didn't know what he was thinking. After ten minutes Master asked him again. He didn't answer. Maybe it was not the time to bother him. "O.K. Vishnu Swami, let us go. I will talk to him tomorrow."

We went to the yoga hall. Master used to sit just at the door between two rows of people: on one side women and on the other side men. As soon as Master came, I took up the *Bhagavad Gita* and read from it and then we dimmed the lantern. There was only the hurricane lamp, and in that dimness, we started to meditate.

Suddenly I heard a noise. I woke from my silent meditation and looked in the direction of the noise. Master was still seated there but someone was beating on his head! I instinctively jumped up. Because I was always with him, it was my natural instinct to protect him. So I went to catch hold of the assailant. I didn't know who he was, or what he was, nothing. We put the lights on and only then did we see it was Govinda. Everyone was stunned.

I saw him hit Master four times on the head. I saw Master looking at Govinda simply, without moving, and Govinda hitting Master's bare head with a big axe! Somehow all the hits missed; it was a miracle. I didn't even know at that time that he was using an axe; I thought he was using a stick. One blow on his bare head should have split the head into pieces. I had enough strength to hold the attacker for the time being. Then I slapped him. It was the first time I actually did that. I'm a swami; I'm not allowed to hit anyone, but I did. It was instinct. Then the whole group, all the devotees, came. They wanted to kill Govinda. Master stood and removed Govinda from the room. He called police headquarters and when an inspector came Master said to him, "Don't do anything to him, just keep him for safe custody tonight, otherwise people will do harm to him. We are going to send him home tomorrow; he is not well." That's all Master said.

It was a very terrible day for us. Our Master just narrowly escaped from an assassin.

The next morning Master walked toward the office as usual, but instead of going there, he gathered some flowers and garlands and fruits. Sometimes in the morning he used to go to the temple so we thought that he was going there because of last night's evil. We followed him, but he didn't go to the temple. He turned towards the police station and went directly to the gate, telling the guard to open it. He asked for the prisoner temporarily staying there. And then he went in to see the would-be assassin!

I will never forget that day. With flowers he garlanded Govinda, his disciple or assassin or whoever he was, and worshipped his feet, dropped flowers on them, and then fell before him as if he were prostrating before God. I remember the humility. He was bowing before an assassin, before a murderer! But Master didn't consider him a murderer. He thought God had come to test him, that God sent this disciple to test him. That's what he felt. He saw God everywhere and that day I saw Master worship his own assassin.

See God in everyone, even in someone who tries to kill you. The same God is in everyone, regardless of how they act.

Ego Fever

In 1949 Sivananda started the Yoga Vedanta Forest Academy, a place where students could come and study various aspects of yoga. He appointed Swamiji to be its professor of hatha yoga. Swamiji was only twenty-one years old and felt totally unequipped to be in such a position.

I liked hatha and raja yoga from the very beginning. When I first met Master, everything came into me; I could do *asanas* and *pranayama* easily. It just came; I didn't learn them like I teach them to you. In fact, they weren't even on the *ashram* program itself because they were not well known any more and not taught very clearly. But Master awakened all my knowledge from past lives enabling me to revive this whole yoga system from the past.

First of all, I didn't have the qualifications to be a professor. I didn't even learn things properly from the Master. I'd only been there for a year and a half. I was a little bit scared because I didn't know what I was going to teach and people kept coming and asking me to teach them. I was not ready; I was still practicing. But Master said, "Don't worry; have faith. You will be ready." That was sufficient. He was behind me the moment I started teaching. Knowledge started pouring in. I knew that someone was there behind me. That was the Master. He, using me, had a way to communicate and to help people. I could feel that, I could answer many questions with answers that amazed me. How could I do that? I was able to switch on somewhere and answers just started pouring forth.

That was Master touching me somewhere. So my body and my mind became an instrument in the hands of my Master to reawaken hatha yoga. In those days I didn't have as much experience as I have now. But slowly, slowly, it came; step by step the methods came, how to devise the poses, how to start, how to finish. So the whole system has been brought completely from my past life experiences and made into a specific method.

Swami Vishnu-devananda was very proud of his position at the *ashram,* but he still looked like a young boy. He felt that he should look the part of a great yogi, so he let his hair and beard grow. Sivananda watched his young student get more and more self-important, and then pricked his balloon with a few simple words. One day he told Swamiji, "Yes, Vishnu Swami, the beard suits you. Yes, it is true, we must all make a good appearance and impress people. Yes, yes, keep on with it."

Swamiji immediately shaved off his beard, and remained clean shaven until late in his life, when he could no longer shave himself. At that point he let his beard grow, rather than trouble his caregivers to shave him every day.

Like his Master, he also became an expert at deflating his students' egos, as the following example illustrates.

> In the summer of 1991 I had the opportunity to serve Swamiji personally. He was in a very weakened condition and was undergoing dialysis treatment. I joined up with Swamiji's team of personal assistants headed by Swami Kartikeyananda and began attending Swamiji during the night. For the next two years until his mahasamadhi I was in Swamiji's presence every night.
>
> To be near him over an extended period of time was the most challenging and stimulating experience of my life. I was constantly baffled by his actions and by the situations arising around him. Nothing seemed to follow logic. As a result, all my preconceptions were shattered. I had to surrender in order to stay near him.
>
> The most striking thing about Swamiji was how he dealt with the ego and its different manifestations in the personality. In front of Swamiji one felt like a child. In my mind there was not a shadow of a doubt that Swamiji saw through me to the deepest recesses of my heart. In front of him I could not pretend I was someone else. I had to be myself.
>
> In the course of my service my ego manifested again and again in different forms, making me identify with the various roles I played in the team of attendants. Swamiji would watch the game of my ego for some time and then all of a sudden, at a time deemed opportune by him, (which was always completely unexpected by me) he would sweep away the whole buildup of my ego.
>
> A few weeks after I began assisting him, Swamiji started peritoneal dialysis. With this new treatment Swamiji did not have to go to the hospital any more for hemodialysis. A special solution was put in his peritoneal cavity for a few hours, drawing the toxins out of his abdomen. The liquid was then drained out and a new solution introduced. The technique was painless but had to be performed regularly four times a day. Swami Kartikeyananda did two exchanges during the day and I was put in charge of the night treatments.
>
> This treatment was vital for Swamiji's life. Any breach in hygienic precautions or lack of attention could cause a fatal infection. I started feeling very important and proud that I had been entrusted with this crucial task. One day at the end of *satsang,* as we were ready to drive home, Swamiji shouted, "Don't think you are a doctor or a nurse." He had to repeat this a few times before I understood. His scolding was totally unexpected because the situation was completely unrelated to any medical procedure. But Swamiji's words went straight to my heart. I realized I was pretending I was somebody else; I was identifying with my role. Swamiji was telling me, "Be yourself!"
>
> Soon after Swamiji left for India. For a few weeks there were many people around him. I noticed that his behavior was different from one disciple to the next. With some people he engaged in friendly conversation, asking questions

and joking. I felt a little jealous. Swamiji never talked to me; to me he would say only the minimum to get what he needed. So one day when I was alone with Swamiji I started to chitchat with him. No sooner had I started than he cut me off. He burst into a sharp, quick scolding. "You talk too much. Say yes or no. That is enough." Again my ego was deflated, but from then on I accepted my silent relationship.

When Swamiji was not traveling he would stay at the Val Morin *ashram* for a few months. He had great difficulty sleeping during the night so he went for long car drives to help him rest. He would instruct us to put on Sant Kesavadas' Devi Mahatmyam tapes and drive to Montreal, about an hour away. We would stop there for a hot drink and a doughnut to keep awake and then drive back to the *ashram*. Sometimes he would go for such drives two or three times a night.

After a few weeks of this routine I began to find the drives a little monotonous and my mind started finding distractions. Sometimes I would drive off the main highway and explore new routes. Swamiji kept silent for a long time, allowing me to become bolder and bolder until I reached the point where I would decide to go this way or that way without asking for permission.

One night Swamiji specifically asked to go to Sainte Agathe for a short drive. He planned to go to Ottawa to visit the yoga center and wished to leave early the next morning. I followed his instructions, but by the time we reached Sainte Agathe he had fallen asleep. We always felt joy when he finally fell asleep. He slept like a baby with a beautiful air of pure innocence on his face. I usually kept on driving until he woke up, so this time I decided to continue on in spite of Swamiji's instructions to just go to Sainte Agathe and come back.

We drove to St. Sauveur and stopped to rest for a few minutes. I fell asleep on the front seat. I woke up to the sound of Swamiji's voice asking, "Where are we?"

I answered "St. Sauveur, Swamiji."

"What! You do what you want? You think you are the big boss now!"

I did not understand why he was scolding me so much. I thought I had been doing the right thing by letting him sleep. But as he kept shouting I realized that he was pointing to that desire to do what I wanted. He made me see clearly how my ego had come up and made me identify with my role as his night driver. I had begun to think I was the one who decided where to go. After that my mind settled down and I was content to go to Montreal and back on the main highway.

Swamiji's scoldings, even though terrifying, were like divine nectar for me—immensely sweet and soothing. They always left me very peaceful, freed from all the tensions created by my mind. The period before the scolding was usually a time of excruciating mental pain where the ego was resisting, rebelling, trying to hold on to its newly-gained territory. During this period Swamiji's attitude was one of complete indifference. Because I had lost tuning with him, I was cut off from his loving energy. After this mental agony it was a great relief to have Swamiji pierce the balloon of my ego, freeing me from the pain.

This period of my life constantly spent in Swamiji's presence has had a deep affect on me. By repeatedly showing me the play of the ego he taught me to be a little more happy in myself.

Swami Atmaramananda

Swamiji's struggle with his own ego was far from over when he shaved off his beard. He continues his narrative of his early years at Sivananda's ashram.

Now I was teaching everyone and it was easy to teach. But what happened to me? See whether I was progressing. What was my main dirt? Was it not ego? The hidden ego was still there. But was I slowly washing it out, or was it building up? It's very difficult to see one's own faults.

I was the hatha yoga professor and Master's personal assistant. I even saved Master's life. All this added to what? My ego started going up. It was really going up now. Apart from my two positions I had to do a lot of work. Life was not easy. We had a limited amount of food and I used to get up in the morning at four o'clock. From then onwards I was continuously working, attending to all my duties and meditations and conducting classes. When everyone went to sleep at night I went to the Ganges to do my own *sadhana* and meditation until twelve o'clock. So I had just a few hours sleep every night. It was extremely difficult.

Apart from all this, ego came. I thought, "I'm here for more than a few years and what am I doing? I'm doing all this work, there's no time for my meditation, no time for my own *asanas*. I can't do my own *pranayama*, my *asanas*; I'm continuously called by duties. This is not a real *ashram*, you know."

My ego grew stronger: "Swami Sivananda is not teaching me everything. He is only asking me to work all the time." I started seeing fault in my own teacher. Slowly, slowly, not only was ego developing but a cloud of doubt arose.

Then, for the first time, Master sent me to represent him. Swami Chidananda and myself were the first to lecture outside the *ashram*. There was a large conference at which we would represent Swami Sivananda. It was a great honor since there were so many other swamis he could have chosen. I had the opportunity to demonstrate *asanas*. Naturally people give great respect to swamis from the Himalayas, especially Swami Sivananda's disciples. So when we went there we had a grand welcome from thousands of people. We got garlanded, we were worshipped; we were lifted up, real gods. We had the best food, the best accommodations, people coming and falling at our feet. I was still only a young man. Can you imagine what a state I was in? What happened further? Ego went up.

Swamiji had mixed feelings about this incident. Swami Chaitanyananda was a contemporary of Swamiji's at the Sivananda *Ashram* in Rishikesh. He remembers that time.

An earnest appeal from the devotees of Jagaadhri in Punjab was made to Guruji to send a few Swamis for a function in their place. The Master chose Chidanandaji for discoursing, Vishnuji for performing asanas and Sharadanandaji for photographing. Assignment completed, they returned and reported to Guruji all that took place, which immensely pleased him.

But strangely it annoyed Vishnuji. He suddenly left the *ashram* and went to a secluded place, Phool Chetti, four kilometers away, beyond Lakshman Jhoola. I felt concerned. I could not figure out the reason for his action. I went to meet and discuss the matter with him.

"I am interested only in Krishna *bhakti* (devotion to Krishna), my *puja* (ritual worship) my *kithidi* (a kind of rice-pudding) and my practice of hatha yoga for myself. I don't want to go out to preach or teach people. Swamiji sent me to Jagaadhri and it greatly disturbed my sadhana. So I came here to do sadhana undisturbed."

"Did you ever give so much as a hint to Guruji that you really dislike doing such things?" I remonstrated with him.

"No," he frankly admitted.

"Then it is not wise to come away like this. You should come back. You have every opportunity to progress spiritually in the *ashram,* but not in this lonely countryside."

"I will come after a few days," he agreed at last.

I left the following day, and, happily, Swami Vishnu returned in two or three days.

It is needless to avert that clearly knowing the future course of his disciple, Guruji was attempting to train him for his future role as a world-famous teacher of yoga. A disciple's knowledge of himself is limited, but the Master's knowledge is thorough and unerring.

Swami Chaitanyanada
Uttar Kashi, India

Swami Vishnu's return was short lived, however, and his mood had not changed.

The day I returned to the *ashram,* the work began again and this and that and this. Master looked at me and saw what was happening in me. This was the time the ego was reaching a dangerous level. It's like a fever, you know. It goes up to 104 degrees and if it goes higher, will kill the person. I went in the evening to take the lantern and do my usual work of leading Master to the office, to the *satsang.* He said, "Vishnu Swami, I don't need your service anymore." He called another swami to do my job for him. "You can go and meditate. I don't need your work now; someone else will do it." That was around eight o'clock in the evening.

You know what that meant? It was the greatest blow I ever had in my life. To get words like that from my Master was not easy to take. That very night, I didn't go to *satsang,* or to meditation. I never missed; I was always with the Master, but tonight another swami came and accompanied Master. I was still in his cottage in the small room which I had been allotted. So I wrote a note saying, "I'm leaving."

That night I left the *ashram*. I had only one set of clothes, a small vessel, and a blanket, but I went wandering in the Himalayas. I walked about fifteen, sixteen miles in the jungle, and stayed all night near a village. The shock was not easy. It was the greatest shock I ever had. I loved my Master very much; I still love him so much. Somehow I displeased him, knowingly or unknowingly. Maybe I wasn't ready to understand him, but he gave me a punishment that I could not take on that day, the greatest punishment.

From then onwards, I entered a new dimension of spiritual life. There was no more support or shade from the teacher. I was alone, trying to find answers, still completely believing in my Master in my heart. I never forgot him; I thought of him more than at any other time in my life. But suffering was there. For more than a year I wandered in search of pilgrims.

Swamiji took up the wandering life. It was not easy. He had no money, and only what he carried with him. Swamiji's cousin tells us what he learned of this time from stories Swamiji told him.

> Someone was always there to help him because his holiness could be vividly recognized. He happened to visit Dwaraka in Gujarat State during the thick of summer. The temperature there was 45 degrees centigrade with no vegetation or shady trees. Even drinking water was very scarce. He came to know about a temple where five sadhus (wandering monks) were fed daily after the midday puja. After a dip in the sea he went to that temple for food but the priest very reverently told him that "biksha that day was already over." He went to the same temple a little earlier the next day, but alas, he had the same fate as the previous day. By then he was totally weary due to hunger, thirst and the prickly weather conditions. He found a thorny tree which gave a little shade, sat under it, and started dozing.
>
> Someone patted him awake and handed him a packet of ground nuts. He ate it greedily; he had nothing the previous two days. By the time he realized that he did not thank his benefactor, the man had already disappeared.
>
> T.L. Nair
> Bombay, India

After his year of wandering, Swamiji returned to the Sivananda Ashram in Rishikesh. He would stay for another seven years, serving his Master, and preparing himself for the next stage of his life.

Early Days

In 1957, twelve years after Swamiji had first come to the *ashram* in Rishikesh, Sivananda told him it was time to leave. "Vishnu Swami, you must go to America. People are waiting there for you to teach them yoga." With his master's blessing and 10 rupees (about $1.00), Swamiji set out. He had never before left India. He spent much of his life either within a ten mile radius of his home village or at the *ashram* in Rishikesh. He knew nothing about life in the West.

He used to tell us that he had to come to the West because many spiritually-inclined souls were reincarnating there. In the West it was much easier for these people to lead a spiritual life. This seemed contradictory to many of us. We thought that you had to go to East, find a teacher, sit in a cave. Swamiji explained that in the West you didn't have to work very hard or very long to get what was needed to lead a simple, healthy life. This left people a great deal of time to pursue spiritual matters. If you were born in the East, in third world and developing countries, most or all of your time would be taken up merely trying to survive.

Swamiji did not travel directly to America. He took a circuitous route, driven by where he could get to next, but always heading towards America. He took each step not knowing how it would lead to the next one, simply having faith that he would get where he was going. At each stop someone, usually a disciple of Sivananda's, would help him organize a few yoga classes to help pay for his ticket to the next place along the way.

> I had just a passport, no money, no sponsors, and a long journey to Ceylon, Singapore, Malaysia, Hong Kong, Australia. I did not know a single person. Finally I arrived in San Francisco at the end of 1957. I spent the New Year and my birthday outside India for the first time. That Christmas I spent in Oakland with the first couple I ever knew.

This couple, Mr. and Mrs. McRury, drove Swamiji into San Francisco every day where he taught classes. Swamiji decided to learn how to drive himself. Earlier on his journey, the Police Chief in Malaysia had given Swamiji an international driver's license, since "everyone in America has a driver's license." Swamiji bought himself an old car and taught himself how to drive in a parking lot. He set off for Los Angeles where the medical department at UCLA paid him $50 per day to undergo various tests. With this money he set off across the United States, heading for New York. In his mind New York defined America. It was the one place in America everyone in India had heard of. He wanted to set up his permanent base there.

With a detour through Eastern Canada, teaching classes in Ottawa and Montreal

Swamiji in Singapore on his way to North America.

along the way, he finally reached New York and started teaching there in the fall of 1958.

Many of his early students have fond memories of these early days.

> Just as I was feeling ready for some good exercise (I didn't know that yoga was any more than that!), a friend told me that India's greatest teacher of hatha yoga had arrived in New York. And so began my first lessons with Swamiji. He sat cross-legged on the bed of his cheap hotel room to leave room for me on the floor. With his yellow pad on his lap, he wrote his *Complete Illustrated Book of Yoga*. Little did I realize that whatever contribution I chose to make may well have made the difference in whether or not Swamiji ate that day. Then came the classes in cheap Broadway rehearsal rooms, walk-up studios, and other affordable spaces until the first fixed Sivananda Yoga Vedanta Center was rented on East 20th Street.
>
> In those days of beginning, I think fondly of the weekends when Swamiji came to our house in the country: my friends, hearing that I was studying yoga, asking only if I could stand on my head or lie on a bed of nails; Swamiji, after an hour-long cocktail and hors d'oeuvres session, exclaiming, when dinner was announced, "You mean that wasn't it?"; a house full of guests protesting that they couldn't possibly stand on their heads and Swamiji promptly standing them on their heads in a row on our dock!
>
> Sylvia K
> New York, NY

ॐ नमो नारायणाय

> I believe it was early in 1959 when I attended a meeting at Carnegie Hall on organic gardening. Next to me sat a woman who raved all evening about a man who was teaching her how to breathe. She was so inspiring that I took all the information necessary to contact this person. The following week I made an appointment to meet this man who called himself Swami Vishnu. We were to meet in a room at a hotel on 23rd Street in New York. My husband and my five-year-old daughter accompanied me on the trip into Manhattan from Long Island.
>
> After locating Swami's room, I knocked and he opened the door. We could see that the room could hardly accommodate three people; it was so tiny. The Swami was a young boy, dark-skinned with a warm smiling face. My husband, being very suspicious, pushed through into the room and sat down. Swamiji offered my little girl an apple and found room in the corner for her. As for me, he asked me to lie face up on the floor and proceeded to instruct me on breathing exercises and a few simple asanas. For several weeks after our first visit we met in this fashion. It was during this time that a center was being formed just a few blocks away.
>
> When our sessions concluded due to the summer season, I asked Swamiji how much I owed him. He told me to beware and if anyone ever asked me for

money in return for services and knowledge, I should run in the opposite direction. He did tell me that I may purchase his book when it was published.

Goodman

New York, NY

Swamiji couldn't stay in New York, however, because he couldn't clear US immigration procedures. He left for Canada, leaving some of his more advanced students to teach classes at the new center. Canadian policy was more favorable to him, probably because he came from a British Commonwealth country, and perhaps because one of his early students was Mrs. Massey, the daughter-in-law of the Governor-General of Canada. Aided by some Jesuit priests, he officially became a Canadian-landed immigrant. He went back to Montreal and started teaching there in early 1959. For the rest of his life he worked out of Montreal and later his ashram in Val Morin, 50 miles north of the city.

Swamiji often told the story of his first year of teaching in Montreal. Classes were going well all through the spring, with many students. Then summer came and suddenly the number of students dropped off dramatically. When he asked where everyone was, he was told that they all went for a vacation in the Laurentian Mountains north of the city. Not one to be deterred, he decided to take his teaching to where the students were.

The first camp started in 1959 in St. Hippolyte, not far from Val Morin. It was in a small cottage belonging to the parents of one of my students. There was no plumbing to supply water; there were just a couple of outdoor toilets and a cottage.

We took a garbage can, made a hole in it, put it on the top of a tree, and then filled it with water to take a shower. There was only one room upstairs. Fifteen women slept upstairs in a small attic and the men slept in the cold Laurentians on the verandah.

It was a three-week camp the first time. When I saw that the people who came to this vacation camp left behind all their luxuries, comforts, and conveniences, and watched how they slept in the attic and on the cold verandah, it opened my heart. I knew that although there were many materialistic attitudes in the West, there were also people who could turn towards an inner world. They knew that there was more than the pursuit of material objects; they took to hard discipline. I realized that here was fertile ground to sow the yogic seed. I knew that even Indians wouldn't take this kind of discipline. They wouldn't do what those students did.

In India, people go to an *ashram* to get blessed and to get hit by peacock feathers. That's all they do. In India they will garland me from head to foot; they'll worship me like a god or an angel, but if I ask them to follow this discipline, no one will come to me. I'm not a miracle maker. I don't care about peacock feathers. I want you all to stand on your own feet to work out your *karma*. That I can show you. That I found in the West.

Swamiji outside the original Montreal Center.

From this first three-week retreat came the idea of people taking yoga vacations. Instead of the usual type of vacation, lost in the pursuit of various pleasures, Swamiji offered people a chance to do intense yoga practice, to really learn by living the practice. Eventually he opened five ashrams: the headquarters in Val Morin, Quebec; in the Catskills in Woodbourne, New York; in the foothills of the Sierras in Grass Valley, California; Paradise Island in the Bahamas; and on top of a hill overlooking a lake in Trivandrum, Kerala, South India. It is interesting to note that, except for the *ashram* in Nassau, which is on a flat coral island, every one of Swamiji's ashrams is in hill country not unlike Sivananda's Rishikesh *ashram* in the foothills of the Himalayas.

> My family is connected with Swami Sivananda and the Divine Life Society in Rishikesh. For ten years in the late 1930's and early 1940's, my father was with Sivananda. Later he returned to South India, took *sanyas*, and worked with poor villagers. My husband and I also met Swami Sivananda in 1961 in Rishikesh. I had heard of Swami Vishnu-devananda while still in India, that he was a disciple of Sivananda's living in the west, in America.
>
> In 1993 my husband and I came to visit my daughter in America. She suggested we go on a tour somewhere, and I said I wanted to go see Swami Vishnu-devananda. We found out that he would be back in Val Morin for the summer so we went to see him in June.
>
> At that time I had the feeling that there was very little difference between the Rishikesh *ashram* and the Val Morin *ashram*. When I woke up in the morning and just opened my eyes, I would often feel that I was in Rishikesh.
>
> Saraswati Devi
> South India

People from all over the world and all walks of life came to the ashrams to learn what Swamiji had to teach. They all went home feeling healthier, more peaceful, and somehow uplifted by the experience.

> Yoga Camp in 1963. The yoga hall was a tiny Quonset hut with no windows. The temperature was in the 50's (fahrenheit) that summer. All the guests took turns doing k.p., setting tables, cleaning the dining room, washing dishes. Swamiji started each day in the yoga hall with a short meditation and long, loud repetition of *Om*. How could we understand the power of the vibrations he was building up for the years to come?
>
> Swamiji taught breathing exercises, eye exercises, and four *asana* classes a day—a beginner's class and an advanced class morning and afternoon. He walked up and down in his bathing trunks and teeshirt, sometimes on his feet, sometimes on his hands! He gave all the lectures. One night he took the whole camp to a nearby French nightclub. "After all," he said, "the people here are only beginners, and you can't expect them to keep their minds always on high spiritual planes. You have to keep them interested."
>
> One afternoon Swamiji called everyone to go for a "little walk."
>
> "Shall we get shoes, Swamiji?"
>
> "No, it doesn't matter. You can come without shoes."

And then a long hike, climbing up and down hills, getting lost in the woods, twisting in and out and over logs and branches and eventually coming back to camp in high spirits, especially those who, as Swamiji knew, would have been sure they couldn't possibly make such a hike!

Swamiji agreed only reluctantly to set a minimum contribution when there was no money to run the camp because people were leaving only a dollar a day or sometimes nothing in donations. In his heart he never abandoned the principle that yoga can neither be bought nor sold; he never turned away anyone who really wanted yoga or needed help, regardless of money.

Sylvia K
New York, NY

ॐ नमो नारायणाय

My closest contacts with Swamiji were in the *ashram* in Val Morin, Canada. I went to the camp year after year during the nineteen sixties and seventies. Once, following the afternoon *asana* class, Swamiji asked how I was enjoying doing the *asanas*. I told him it was like the old Listerine advertisement: I hate it twice a day. I always knew how to make him laugh.

One year as I was saying good-bye, preparing to return to New York, he asked how I'd enjoyed the stay at the camp. I told him that for the entire two weeks, all I could think about was going home. He looked disappointedly towards the ground until I added that for the next fifty weeks at home, all I would think about was next year's return. You should have seen the smile on his face!

Thomas Zepler
Brooklyn, NY, USA

ॐ नमो नारायणाय

My late wife, Theresa, induced me to accompany her to the Val Morin *ashram*, where we arrived on Aug. 1, 1967. On that day, after hearing Swamiji talk about the evils of smoking and the advantages of vegetarianism, I gave up any form of tobacco forever and became a vegetarian, although I had smoked a pipe, cigars, and cigarettes for over thirty years and had always eaten meat.

I owe Swamiji an eternal debt of gratitude, for I am convinced that except for him, I would not have reached, in good health, my present age of 91.

Leo Silverstein
New York, NY, USA

ॐ नमो नारायणाय

There was a woman here, a celebrity. We were all sitting with Swamiji, telling him what a great yoga camp it was and how much we were benefiting by it. Quite a few people came because they were physically ill. Quite a few people came with other problems. The elegant lady from New York joined us as we were chronicling our sorrows and troubles and said arrogantly, "Well, I'm happy. I have no problems." Swamiji knew she was very privileged and very talented. He looked her straight in the eye and said, "If you didn't have problems and you were completely happy, you wouldn't be here."

Neela Devi
Washington, DC, USA

ॐ नमो नारायणाय

I'll never forget the first time I met Swami Vishnu. At Christmas my husband and I had come with trepidation to the yoga retreat on Paradise Island for the first time. We soon fell in love with that inner feeling of peace, with yoga, and with the incredibly beautiful setting. We couldn't wait to come back four months later, for the Easter conference, when Swami Vishnu would be there.

In the interim, a fellow guest at the retreat told us to go study in New York City with a venerable old yogi. There we went all fresh and eager and enthusiastic. We started to attend his yoga classes, which were strenuous and exhilarating. Then we told him we wanted to study *pranayama* and meditation. He took us into his inner sanctum, his private meditation area, and told us it would cost us $501 cash each for *pranayama* lessons, and $501 cash each for meditation. For those fees he would work with us as long as we needed. Needless to say, the price dampened our ardor. Eventually this wily old yogi offered a *pranayama* class for all his students at a regular price, which we attended with curiosity, distrust, and reservations.

With this experience as background, we arrived at the yoga retreat for the Easter conference. One afternoon, amidst fanfare and excitement, announcements were made that Swami Vishnu was going to give a *pranayama* class for all guests. Everyone assembled at the tennis court, at least a hundred people. There was a great air of anticipation and elation.

Swami Vishnu bustled in, bringing tremendous energy. We were astounded with the class. He couldn't give us enough; his generosity was overflowing. He wanted to impart as much knowledge as possible. He took us through *kapalabhatti* and *anuloma viloma* practices and was ready to go on to more advanced practices. My husband and I were stunned. In one two-hour session, we learned more than in all the time we had spent with that other yogi. What a difference! Night and day!

Swami Vishnu inundated us. Instead of being students trying to pry knowledge from an unwilling source, we were now students with the delightful problem of how to take it all in. From starvation to feasting! It was all there, available to us, being offered to us, even more, being handed to us! We had gone from being treated like Cinderella to being welcomed guests at the table of the proverbial Jewish grandmother. How much we could take in depended only on our capacity to receive and retain.

Martha Gunzburg
New York, NY, USA

ॐ नमो नारायणाय

When the pupil is ready the teacher will appear, and sometimes we are led to our destiny in the most unlikely places.

I first met Swami Vishnu in 1963. I was taking yoga classes at the YWCA in New Haven, Connecticut. Our teacher was excellent. I was most impressed with her ability to induce complete relaxation. Where did she learn this? "Oh," she replied, "don't go there. It's a little town in the middle of nowhere, in Canada. There's nothing to do at night, no nightclubs, no dancing!" So off I went to the Yoga Camp in Val Morin, Quebec. I took leotards and fancy clothes. If it was a failure, I'd drive down to the Maine beaches.

Frankly, I was not prepared for my reception at the camp. Swamiji, a small, dark man in red swim trunks, was sitting on his favorite rock talking with a guest. He got up and ran down the hill, bare feet and all, to greet me. One of the things that impressed me most then and later was that he never asked me what I did for a living or any of the other probative questions we take for granted. He just took people as they were.

He told me that the new lodge was built but didn't have toilets yet. I could sleep in a cottage if I preferred. It was not the Hilton. I later learned that my roommate was a health freak who stayed up all night crunching on carrots and running out to the bathroom to perform various inner cleansings. After a night on a mattress that felt like an egg crate, I had made up my mind. I'd head for the Maine coast in the morning.

I went to the yoga hall for morning meditation. Swamiji had scrambled up the hill from his hut, still in his red shorts, but he threw orange robes over them. As he settled himself on the stage I looked around. Everyone had their eyes closed, so I closed mine. And the rest, as they say, is history.

Swamiji was omnipresent, switching from his meditation role as spiritual leader by jumping off the stage to teach us *asanas*, demonstrating them perfectly. He circulated around the room, trailing a cloud of soothing energy as he went. You would be almost tempted to make a mistake just to win his attention. Humor was always part of the process. It was nothing to hear Mrs. Peyser yell, "Swami, Swami, don't leave me! as she swayed in the headstand and to hear Swamiji chuckling, "I'm right here" as he walked away, leaving her in mid-air.

We all ate together, Swamiji at the head of the table. One of my first vivid memories was when he handed me a plate of table scraps and told me to go down the hill and feed the goat. Who? Me? A hotshot Connecticut educator should approach Kiddie, his pet goat? We had to be careful with Kiddie, but Swamiji would romp with him, pretend to butt heads, and then turn and make Kiddie chase him.

Swamiji was playful, at times almost child-like. He never called us by our given names. I was "Kon-nek-ti-kut" or "New Heaven." How I longed to have him call me Alice. When he finally did, I was sorry because it was "Alice do this, Alice do that."

Life with Swamiji wasn't all fun and games. He taught karma yoga, the yoga of selfless service. We had plenty of work to do around the camp. Swamiji practiced what he preached; he came and helped, tugged, pulled, and chopped. I painted everything that didn't move. Everyone helped in the kitchen. The meals often got less luxurious when we owed the local grocer. Swamiji was extremely generous and would never turn anyone away. Since contributions for stays were completely voluntary and really fluctuated, managing the budget was never easy.

The last morning of my stay I sat in meditation. Tears filled my eyes. Swamiji saw my distress and asked someone to pack up a tin of cookies for me, as if to send a little child away happy. As I drove down the highway the sad tears became tears of joy as I sang, "Om Namah Sivaya." I was happy I had discovered yoga.

Alice Frazier
Woodmont, CT

Peace Missions

Swamiji was a great activist for world peace. From the late 1950's onward he was constantly looking for ways to bring to the world's attention the need for peace on earth, and to demonstrate practical ways to achieve this peace. He was always alert for an opportunity to go on another peace mission.

His primary way of catching people's attention was by flying peace missions in his peace planes—first a twin engine Piper Apache and later an ultralight. He would fly over the world's trouble spots, often at great personal risk to himself, "bombing" these places with leaflets and flowers. Through these flights he became known as "The Flying Swami."

Why did he do this? What drove him to repeatedly risk his life and reputation? He explained it this way.

> In the *ashram* in Nassau I had a powerful vision. It shook me and even several hours after that vision, I could not think properly. I realized that if and when the vision materialized, it would be the most difficult thing in my life. I had no idea how or when it would happen. A voice came to me telling me to fly. I had no idea why, but the voice said yes. So for many years I flew, going through all the criticism, ("the Swami is flying"), so much criticism about the luxury of a private plane. Still I did not really understand why I had to fly. I thought perhaps for freedom, perhaps against war. But now I see that all my years of flying really had only one purpose: to break the boundaries of passport and visa. When you are on the ground the authorities can stop you at the border, but when you are up in the air, no one can stop you. Either they have to shoot you down or they have to let you land. There is no other choice for any government.
>
> And so, the boundary breaking mission came. It demonstrated symbolically to the world that the planet is small. Either we are going to live together or we are going to die together. The time has come for the idea of nationalism, of patriotism, to disappear, and for only unity to exist.

Swamiji prepared for his peace missions through the early months of 1971 by upgrading his aircraft, a Piper Apache, putting in extra fuel tanks and special long-range radio equipment. The outside of the plane was also prepared. Peter Max, an artist of the era, painted the exterior in a bright 'pop' style. Swamiji also created a

Planet Earth Passport for himself and his traveling companions, symbolically stating that they weren't from any specific country or region or nationality. His passport information read as follows:

Name - Swami Vishnu-devananda, randomly born on the Earth
Date of Birth - Immortal
Residency - Earth
Weight - Immeasurable
Height - short as well as tall, big as well as small
Hair - snow white
Eyes - intuitive
Present address: Street - Planet Earth; City - Vaikuntha; State - God.

Swamiji in the cockpit of his peace plane.

Swami Vishnu-devananda on his private airplane.

His first stop was going to be Belfast, Northern Ireland, then in the thick of an undeclared civil war, and occupied by British troops. The actor, Peter Sellers, had agreed to meet him in Dublin.

On September 5th, Peter Sellers came to the hotel in Dublin. We had a first meeting about how we were going to start our boundary breaking mission. The date of September 8th had already been selected. It was an auspicious day because it was Master Sivananda's birthday. That is why I wanted to start the peace mission on September 8th.

It so happened that that day was Peter Sellers birthday too. He promised me, "Swamiji, I will do anything for you and for the peace mission."

So I said, "Why don't you come and fly with me to Belfast? We will go and do some chanting, and drop some flowers and leaflets, and do the first ever peace bombing in a country."

He agreed, but said he had to consult with his wife, lawyer, business associates, and so forth. At least he gave a tentative answer: he would try to help. I said we could decide the next day. Meanwhile he could contact his press agent in London to help us with the London press conference planned for the next day.

The next day I flew from Dublin to London. I arrived at London airport where all our staff was waiting. It was a wonderful day; the press conference was well attended. First we gave the preliminary publicity and press information to the public and various stations. The press was asking whether Peter Sellers was coming, and I said, "Yes, he is coming and he is not coming", because I did not want to give him advance publicity. I was quite sure he still had to contact his wife and I knew there was something wrong.

During the press conference itself, I had a long-distance call from Peter: "Swamiji, I do not think it is worthwhile for me to come to Belfast. My business manager and agents all think it is a very dangerous game, going to Belfast, where they are shooting Londoners."

He was from London and Irish people don't like Londoners. So they scared him. He was afraid that by going into the street he would get shot, so his agents were advising against his going to Northern Ireland. So I said, "O.K., if you think so, it is all right. Anyhow, I will see you in Dublin before I take off for Belfast." He actually wanted to come but the other people scared him so much he did not know what to do.

I flew back to Dublin. Peter had made all the hotel arrangements and covered all our expenses. He came to the hotel and met me again saying, "Swamiji, I think I've changed my mind; I want to come with you."

"I think that is the right thing to do," I said. "but think about it twice, because of the danger in the street." You know, they were shooting everyone there.

That evening I came down to the lobby from my room, and Peter Sellers was there with quite a few people with him. I said, "What are you doing here, Peter?"

"Oh, Swamiji," he said, "I am trying to make my will". He called his lawyers and business managers and made his will in case something happened to him. Do see his sincerity? That is the thing, you know. In spite of all the risk, he wanted to come.

So I said, "Peter, nothing is going to happen to you. It is your birthday, and Master is going to help you too." Then I said good-bye, until the next morning.

We met at the airport. By that time the press heard that Peter Sellers was coming so they all came too. We prepared our "bomb" for bombarding Belfast: lots of flowers and specially printed leaflets. I had sent a student ahead to Belfast to make sure people would know we were coming there in case we got shot.

We got into the aircraft and tried to arrange our bomb; it was our first peace-bombing and we did not know how to handle everything. We put everything near my left window so that I could release the flowers. Bren, my co-pilot, was sitting at my right. We took off, and soon arrived above Belfast. The weather was a little hazy over the city. There were some mountains ahead, and as I came down over the mountains the city could be seen in half-haze. I had seen Belfast two years before when I was there on a peace march and did some chanting, so I knew a little bit about the Belfast area. But from the air it was quite new.

Due to the haze I could not see well. We planned to bomb the City Hall first. We did not have a proper map of the Belfast area, so I was using my memories from two years ago: "It must be somewhere in that area." I came down to about 1000 feet, but was still not sure, so I called the Belfast control tower. I told them we were just above such and such a place, and could they please tell us how we could locate City Hall?

They knew the plane was coming, but they answered, "We are unable to give you that information."

So I called again: "Charlie Fox here. Could you please tell us where the main street is?"

And again they answered, "Charlie Fox we are unable to give you your exact location. Please report your altitude and your speed."

I answered, "We are at about 1,000 feet," because that was the limit; we should not be below 1000 feet. This is a rule. I was actually a little bit lower. I thought our present location was just above the palace area. They further asked what was our estimated arrival time at the airport. So I said, "I'll call you back; standby."

At last I located the main road. Bren was beginning to collect all the leaflets. Peter was at my right. I put the plane a little bit more into position and dove down towards main street. We began bombing all over Belfast. The leaflets and flowers were flying everywhere; they were all over! It was a beautiful sight, like white doves everywhere.

After the bombing we called the tower again. "Charlie Fox. We are at such and such place. Please give instructions for landing." And he gave us a runway number where we landed.

The police and other officials were all waiting for us. But suddenly, on the runway, the leaflets began coming out of everywhere. When you are bombing for the first time, you do not know where all the bombs will go. Where were all these leaflets coming from? We realized that some had gotten caught in the tail of the plane. It was a violation because it could be a traffic hazard. I called the tower and said, "No, sir, this is not intentional. Some of the leaflets we dropped got stuck in the tail. We were not aware of this. Please report to the authorities, if this is any violation."

The officials asked for our passports; we showed our Planet Earth Passports and they were very kind. One officer said, "You know, you violated the regulations. It is a hazard to drop leaflets from the air."

I replied, "I know sir, but war is still more of a hazard. We threw only leaflets and flowers."

He said it was just a formality but, "We have to warn you." He had to do his duty, you see. Customs officials came and stamped our passports then asked for autographs from Peter Sellers and from me. They were very courteous.

After this we had to get the plane nearer to the fence because the TV people were already waiting outside. I brought the plane close to them so that they could take pictures.

Peter Sellers and I held a conference and decided to go into the city, so we drove by car to the city, chanting Hare Ram and Sita Ram, and Jesus Krishna is Thy Name, Love Thy Neighbor as Thyself. That was our song. So we were singing and dropping leaflets from the car as we went.

Our first stop was the place where soldiers waited, where the Catholic-Protestant junctions are, a kind of no man's land. Catholics were on one side, Protestants on the other. Two years before I had done chanting there so we made that our first stop. There was a big mob of people but we did not feel any hostility. They were running after Peter Sellers and getting autographs; it was a very wonderful scene. We gave leaflets to all the people including the soldiers.

Our next stop was to see the mother and the father of the three months old baby shot by a sniper bullet. It was really a tragic thing to happen to this young couple, both in their twenties. At the time of the shooting the baby was being taken for a walk by her sister, a five year old child. They were walking on the street when suddenly a bullet grazed the five-year-old, but only at the skirt. But the three-month-old baby was not lucky. She was killed instantly. The five year old wheeled her into the house, dead.

We went into their house not knowing what kind of reception we would find. We recognized the couple and they recognized us; some other local people were also there. We prayed for their peace.

Next stop was to Ian Paisley, the Protestant minister. I met him two years before when he invited me to his church. That church is used mainly for political purposes; there is no spirituality there. Several American business people supported this church financially. The whole church was completely polluted by political thoughts. People are gullible and Paisley could agitate them, just like Hitler could. So militant. But anyhow, he was nice to me that first time.

This time we drove to his house but his wife said, "He is not at home. He drove to the Parliament." So we went to the Parliament: Peter Sellers, myself, and the whole group, including newspapermen. They were all running. When we came to the place he was not there. We tried to see the Prime Minister, but he was out of town, too. So we just sat down and started chanting *Hare Rama*. After fifteen minutes we saw Paisley come in. We went inside to catch him, but he had a meeting with a minister. There was some televising going on at the ministry, so all he said was, "Hello, good-bye" and left. He did not want to talk to us; he was afraid. So we took off to Dublin that same day.

That was our first peace mission.

For the rest of his life Swamiji went on one peace mission after another. He constantly spoke out against sectarian violence and man-made divisions. Some of his peace missions, like his flight from Tel Aviv to Cairo in 1971, and his flight over the Berlin Wall in an ultra light plane in 1983, received a great deal of attention in the press. Others went almost unnoticed. It made no difference to him; he was only doing his duty. The results he left up to God.

In November 1989, Swamiji made arrangements to visit Israel. This was still a dangerous period. The Palestinian uprising (Intifada) continued in the occupied territories of the Mideast with daily stone throwing and unrest. For his love of humanity Swamiji had no fear at all in visiting these territories on one of his incomparable flower and peace leaflet bombings.

Three cars full of enthusiastic (but rather nervous) yoga students arrived with Swamiji at the military guard to Kalkiliya, a small town on the West Bank of the Jordan River. The contingent of 16 people was comprised mainly of Israeli nationals and they weren't sure how the inhabitants of the town would react to them. Already negative reports were coming through the media telling the public to avoid such areas. But Swamiji was with us and his presence was like a granite rock. What harm could there be?

It took about half an hour for the soldiers to complete all formalities and soon we were all led into the village by two military jeeps. Once in the village, despite the quietness of kafiya-crowned Arabs slowly milling around we felt a rather eerie vibration. After a left turn and a few blocks down the road we parked the vehicles and carefully emerged into an unknown environment, a potential death trap. The streets were lined at short intervals with Israeli soldiers, heavy and dangerous rifles hanging from their shoulders. We were told not to depend only on the soldiers to protect us as just the day before they themselves were victims of vicious stone throwing.

The first thing Swamiji did was to enter a pharmacy near the parked cars. His exuberance took the proprietors by surprise and soon the flowers and pamphlets were delivered. It was fortuitous that they knew English well and Swamiji could easily explain his purpose which was happily accepted. A spirit of friendship and love was already created. Out in the street now, Swamiji (walking with difficulty due to body ailments) led his band of colorfully dressed disciples (some were swamis wearing orange, others brahmacharis wearing yellow) to each person he met. Personally the flowers were offered and pamphlets distributed. Each individual was literally taken by surprise. But it was clear that we were there on genuine grounds and it was obvious by now that we were not typical folk coming to cause trouble. After "conquering" a few blocks Swamiji sat down on a small traffic island in the middle of the street and, as the disciples followed suit, he began chanting aloud for peace. Soldiers watched smilingly and with some amusement, if not incredulity.

Looking up the street one could feel the powerful vibration set up by Swamiji. One could hardly believe any longer that this was a battle field. As the chanting continued two young Arab girls shyly approached Swamiji. One, a journalist, began to complain to him how badly the Israeli government was treating them. In a loving way Swamiji brushed the complaints aside and handed to her a copy of The Complete Illustrated Book of Yoga. She started to leaf through it with interest.

Swami Padmapadananda

Swamiji also spoke constantly throughout the 1970's and 1980's about the threat of a nuclear holocaust. He was always reminding us that the world, and our own lives, could end at any moment. Some people thought he was being morose and gloomy when he did this. Actually he was just trying to spur us on to more vigorous spiritual practice, more *sadhana.* "Don't wait for tomorrow. There may be no tomorrow. Start today. Take advantage of every moment."

I remember that at one yoga retreat I was invited to have lunch with Swamiji. After we were seated and after greetings I asked Swamiji if I could ask three questions. He broke out in a big smile, laughed, and replied "Of course."
My first question was, "Were we all going to be blown up in a nuclear war?"
He gave a quick answer. "Probably."
The second question was, "Is there any hope?"
"Yes, there is always hope."
The third question was, "What can we do?"
"We can help each person in front of us, one at a time."

Bill Forster
Silver Springs, MD, USA

In 1987, the 100th anniversary of Sivananda's birth, Swamiji and 60 other pilgrims went to India on the Sivananda Centennial Tour. The focus of the trip was the Peace Mala that Swamiji had organized. We were to join hands with thousands of people forming a human necklace that would extend from Rishikesh, where Master Sivananda's *ashram* is located, to the sacred city of Haridwar, a distance of about thirty miles. Chanting the mantra *Om Namo Narayanaya,* we would draw down Lord Narayana's preserving energy, and so further world peace. The following are memories of that day.

Swamiji told us that the day of the Peace Mala was the most important day of his life. He said that if it went off successfully, he would consider his life work done. He hoped soon to leave his body, he told us, but promised to save a place for us, "rent free," in his new abode.

So it was with a real sense of mission that we rose early this morning and headed for Haridwar, where we were to make up the end of the Mala which began in Rishikesh. We arrived at 9:30 in the morning and trooped across a filthy stretch of muddy no man's land to the famous bridge over the Ganges. It overlooks the sacred bathing ghats. While on our previous visit to Haridwar we had struggled through a barricade of leprous, maimed beggars, now we were to remain on the bridge, in their midst, for hours. The prospect wasn't just disheartening, it was terrifying. I think we all wondered wistfully, "Why has Swamiji sent us here? Why can't we be in Rishikesh, where it's pleasant and clean and we're surrounded by nice people?"

At 11 o'clock we joined hands and started chanting. Just then the sun came out and began to beat down on us mercilessly. I started to worry about getting heat prostration again; earlier in my trip it really wiped me out. A number of beggars joined hands with us. I was holding hands with a tiny, beautiful, little girl. Was she a beggar or just a street urchin, I wondered. And what's the difference between a beggar and a street urchin? Eventually I noticed that except for the beggars, nobody in Haridwar had turned out to join us. In fact, the line just barely straggled across the bridge.

Did this mean the Mala was a failure? We had no way of knowing. Perhaps it was more successful at its other points, perhaps not. Still, we had good *shakti* (spiritual energy) as we chanted, despite the groups of beggars pestering us. But when a band of lepers drifted toward me, and then stopped right in front of me to have an animated conversation, I was seized by raw terror and revulsion. How could I pray for world peace, when all I wanted was for the lepers to go away?

Then, at about 11:40, I remembered the limes. Swami Sitaramananda had told me to buy enough for everybody so that we could cut them and squeeze them into our throats to help ease our hoarseness. I was passing around the limes when Swami Sitaramananda collared me and a few other tour members and took us to a point quite near the end of the line, where most of the mendicants and *sadhus* were and the chanting was weak.

I had no idea how I could help pick up the chanting at this end of the line when I was now almost voiceless. And I knew I couldn't take the sun much longer. But I took my place. I had half a lime in my pocket and I squeezed it into my open mouth. A big squirt of lime juice hit the back of my throat like a bull's eye. Suddenly my voice came back completely, all my cold symptoms vanished, and I was chanting *Om Namo Narayanaya* at the top of my lungs in a crystal clear voice. Around me, I could hear my fellow chanters; their energy also had intensified. What was more, I had a distinct sensation of coolness. Tiny cool breezes seemed to be wafting around us. This went on for several minutes, during which time we all chanted with tremendous energy.

It was now 12:20. Swamiji was expected any minute; he was supposed to drive along the Mala from Rishikesh to Haridwar. In fact, he'd been due at noon. The chanting ended except for a small group, and we were mobbed by angry beggars who'd expected to be fed. Exhausted, I sat with a group of others from the tour in the shade of the nearby stalls, and gulped down soft drinks. Morale was low. Swamiji didn't arrive until 2:00.

Because of the delay in Swamiji's arrival in Haridwar some of us feel very ill-used. But in the three years that I've been privileged to know Swamiji, he's never been even remotely on schedule. I know that the blessings of today will be with me in lifetimes to come, despite, or maybe because of, the hardships we endured. That is surely more important than being on schedule.

Saraswati
New York, NY

ॐ नमो नारायणाय

I had been assigned the task of video cameraman for the 1987 Centennial Tour. On the day of the Peace Mala I was supposed to film the entire length of the mala from its start in the plaza in front of Sivananda's Mahasamadhi shrine in Rishikesh to its end at the ghats in Haridwar.

Earlier in the morning I had been in the main hall where all the senior disciples of Sivananda, including Swamiji, were performing pada puja to silver replicas of Sivananda's sandals. Thousands of people were gathered chanting "Om Namo Bhagavate Sivanandaya" as the sandals were buried in a mound of flower petals. I could see that if they were really going to repeat the mantra 10,008 times that they would never be finished by 11:00, when the procession from Rishikesh to Haridwar was supposed to start. I left to set up my camera in the plaza, assuming Swamiji would soon follow.

I met with Swami Shanmugananda and one or two other senior staff who were organizing the Rishikesh end of the mala. They had gathered a small crowd of sanyasins and we formed a line from the Mahasamadhi shrine, across the plaza and down a long flight of steps to the main road. At 11:00 we started chanting Om Namo Narayanaya, initially with a lot of energy, but gradually our energy flagged. I had only been in India a week or so, and hadn't yet given up my North American idea of promptness. Instead of just letting go and chanting until he came I mentally worried and grumbled about Swamiji being "late again".

By 11:45 I was quite frantic. We were supposed to be in Haridwar at noon. It was 30 miles away on mediocre roads, and we hadn't even started yet. By this time I had enough film of the start of the mala, and had gone down to the bottom of the stairs by the road, wanting to make sure I caught Swamiji. At 11:50 he came roaring by mounted on a float built on the back of a flatbed truck. He went right by me without stopping, but a car carrying a few other people stopped and I piled in.

I filmed out of the window of the car as it whipped along on the road into Rishikesh, a mile or so away. Huge bands of school children lined the roads in their uniforms, chanting Om Namo Narayanaya as we went whizzing by. The people on the truck and all of us in the car chanted along with them.

Suddenly we stopped at the gates of a Sikh *ashram* on the outskirts of town. Swamiji had been taking extra care to include the local Sikhs in everything we did in Rishikesh. This was three years after he had tried to mediate between Sikhs and the Indian government in Amritsar, just before the Golden Temple massacre. "This was just going to make us even later," I thought, still not tuned in to what was really important.

I jumped out of the car to film the meeting between Swamiji and the Sikh leaders, which consisted mainly of many pranams and hugs and a few words. Then Swamiji climbed back up on the truck, motioning me to get up beside him. Now we drove down the main market street of Rishikesh, driving more slowly because of the crowds, and still chanting. There were definite breaks in the chain, and many people stared at us in open amazement as we drove by.

As we drove through the city we were joined by a young man on a motor scooter, riding along beside us, smiling and chanting. Before we knew it, we were surrounded by thirty or forty motorcycles ridden by one or two young men each. As we pulled out of Rishikesh and picked up speed they all stuck with us, riding up along both sides of the truck, weaving in and out amongst each other and positively shouting the chant.

There were now long stretches in the open country where there was no chain at all. As we pulled in to each village along the way there would be another long line of school children and their teachers waiting for us. By now we were very late, so we barely slowed down. I wondered what they would think of us. They had waited for well over an hour and all they saw was a truck and a car packed with people, Swamiji mounted on a large chair on the back of the truck, surrounded by wild young men on motorcycles, all chanting themselves hoarse as they zipped by.

As we reached the edge of Haridwar, a train barrier came down across the road, stopping us dead in our tracks. All the young men got off their motorcycles and jumped up and down around the truck and Swamiji, still chanting. I realized at this point that they were all pronouncing the mantra incorrectly, leaving off the last syllable. There we were, later than ever, surrounded by what looked like a bunch of partying teenagers. Swamiji just sat still and calm, chanting, seemingly unmoved by the craziness all around us.

Finally the train barrier went up, we rushed into Haridwar, parked behind the ghats and hurried to the water's edge. I was exhausted by the emotion of the event and the heat and humidity, but Swamiji was just getting going. He rushed down the steps of the ghat, followed by our motorcycle gang escort, who I'm sure had little idea of what this was all about. He stood up to his knees in the Ganges and started saying some Sanskrit prayers. We were surrounded by not only the people we'd come with, but the people who had been waiting for us here all this time, plus many others who just happened to be at the ghats. Everyone was shoving and pushing to get close to Swamiji and hear and see what was going on. Somehow an arati lamp appeared and we performed *arati* to Mother Ganga.

Swamiji sat on the steps of the ghat and started to talk. The motorcycle boys became very still and quiet and listened intently. The first thing Swamiji did was teach them how to pronounce *Om Namo Narayanaya* correctly, going over it a syllable at a time, gradually getting them to repeat it correctly along with the rest of us. He then gave a talk. I honestly can't remember a word he said. I was so struck by how our wild escort was now sitting so still, listening to Swamiji. If nothing else had happened, these young men had somehow been reached by Swamiji in some way.

Was the Peace Mala a success? I have no way of judging. It had been one of the most frantic and crazy days of my life. In the midst of all it Swamiji was a calm center, doing what he felt he had to do. After the lecture, he sat all by himself on the ghat steps and meditated. He radiated peace.

Gopala Krishna

Mantra Initiation

Swami Vishnu-devananda's philosophy of life was evident in everything he did. He believed, lived, and taught that one person could make a huge difference in the lives of others. Because he was a link in the ancient lineage chain of yoga, he also passed on the great powers of yoga initiation. Swamiji spoke on this subject often.

Initiation literally means "ignition." When you start a fire, how do you start it? You start with small little twigs and papers; you ignite the twigs and then slowly add larger wood and soon you have a huge fire! But how much fire did you use to start it? One small match stick, is it not? A small match stick is able to ignite that hidden energy in the firewood. Fire comes from that. We are all nothing but dormant energy. Like the firewood, fire is still there, but in a dormant state. The wood which has gone into the fire becomes part of the fire and increases the energy. That's the whole secret of the initiation. Initiation means using the mantra as a way to enlighten your heart, or to lighten your heart.

Even before the earth was born, mantra energy was in a certain state. Newton did not create gravity. He discovered the existence of an energy called gravity. It was not new when Newton discovered it. Nor did Edison create electricity. Electricity was there. Edison discovered the existence of a certain energy called electricity. In the same way, this mantric energy existed, even before creation.

Everything is in a state of vibration; everything is energy waves. Your body also vibrates at a specific wavelength. You learn to tune to specific wavelengths to get a specific energy or strength or power. Mantra is a particular wavelength of a spiritual mystical symbol. Eventually your mind will be tuned to it. At that time you will have cosmic consciousness or meditation. That's the secret formula.

Each individual must have a mantra to suit his particular mind. But we can't have four billion mantras. For four billion people we don't cook four billion different types of food.

What type of food do you have? One type of food you like much better than another, is it not? What did they serve for breakfast? Granola, fruit, bread and butter, and yogurt. Some of you took more granola; some took more butter and more bread; some took more yogurt, is it not? Though we have been given the same food, one food you like much better than another. But the purpose is what? To nourish your body, you take granola, more and more.

It is the same with mantras. There is no such thing as a superior mantra or inferior mantra. All mantras are alike, are equal and have equal efficiency. Just like fire; all fire burns. Of course, some wood can burn more, if it's not wet. But even the wet wood will burn.

In India we know which mantra is suitable to a particular mind, because we know the deities. Every name has got a form; every form has got a name. We cannot use any word as a mantra; the form of the word you use will be reflected in your mental state. According to the yoga psychology, your mind assumes the form of the objects you think of or meditate on. If you are thinking of an orange your mind takes the shape of the orange in order to have the perception of the orange. This is the law; this you must remember very clearly. So if I'm thinking orange, orange, orange, the mind takes the shape of the orange. Then only is visibility and perception possible. If there is no form of the orange, even if you're repeating "orange, orange, orange, orange, orange, orange, orange," if there's no form, it has no impact on the mind. The mind doesn't know what it is; it's just a word.

In the same way, form alone is not sufficient. If you just visualize the form without the orange name then the form has no effect on the mind. You need name and form. If you want to see the fire, but there is no form of fire in your mind, you can repeat "fire, fire." Still you cannot think of the fire. Name and form go together.

If this were not so, you could use any word for meditation. You can use "flower, flower, flower, flower, flower, flower, flower, " but your body and mind cannot be lifted by a flower, the energy coming from the flower, the radiation from the flower. The wavelength of the flower and the object flower have no permanent impact on your mind. Only spiritual words can lift you up. These words are called spiritual mantras.

The Supreme Being is one and is called OM. The highest mantra is OM: A - U - M. All other mantras emanate from this OM: A - U - M. Every mantra that we can speak of, and every language in fact, is hidden in this one cosmic syllable OM. The meaning of that OM syllable is very difficult for the ordinary mind to grasp. For this reason we very seldom initiate anyone into OM, though it is highest mantra. Because people don't have the highest subtle intellect to meditate on an abstract form like OM, but still you can meditate on OM if you want. There's no harm, because it is abstract. All other mantras are concrete, they have a specific name or form.

Are you a Krishna type, a Rama type, a Siva type or a Devi type? These are the basic personality types.

Are you a family person, a householder, interested in wife or husband, children, a nice steady healthy family, family unity? You want peace in the family and a real relation to your husband or wife, a spiritual relation. You think that children should respect their parents. If that's the type of life you are more engrossed by, then you have the Rama type personality. Rama is the embodiment of that character, he is the embodiment of the ideal husband, ideal child, ideal god and ideal destroyer of the demons and establisher of law and order. He is an ideal in everything, perfect. He has only one wife for his whole life. In all his life he never even looked at another woman. He has only one wife and that's all, that's his whole attitude. So this attracts real family types and those who handle the family responsibilities. If you have a character like that, then you meditate on Rama. You should be initiated into a Rama mantra.

Others are withdrawn types. They will go to Mount Kailas, like Lord Siva, perpetually in the snow-capped mountains, away from the hustle and bustle. In the snowy peaks Lord Siva lives and meditates. Any devotee interested will come to him; he is not interested in running towards the devotee. He's another withdrawn type. If you have that type of attitude, even if you are a family member, or a householder, or a business person, if your temperament is more removed and it doesn't make any sense to you to get too much into the active social life and running towards social things; you want to be quiet and relaxed in attitude and withdrawn, then you should be initiated into a Siva mantra.

The greatest majority of the people are Krishna types. Krishna has all the characteristics of every human being from childhood onwards to a very advanced age. In one life, he played every part we can think of. He was a statesman, teacher, king and player. Anything you can think of, he had the ability to show it in himself, in one life. So the vast majority of people like that particular temperament because of the various characters Krishna played. We give the Krishna mantra if you have a temperament like that.

Others are more interested in the Mother. They have more affinity to the divine creative power and energy. They've got more love and compassion, like a universal mother and they are more close to the Mother's heart. God also manifests as mother, not only as father. He has all the aspects, the feminine too. Then we can meditate on this aspect by getting a mantra of Durga or Devi.

Once you have chosen a deity and a mantra and a *guru*, don't change this all your life. You don't change the mantra; you don't change your teacher; you don't change your deity. This is for your whole life. If you are going to get initiation, do not try to change or find another mantra. It's no good for you. If you don't have belief in your teacher, then don't take mantra from that teacher. Try to find a teacher in whom you have belief and faith. You have to have certain feelings for the teacher to get the benefit of the initiation. Then only can the teacher ignite you.

It's not a commercial mantra we are giving. We are not interested to take any money or anything from you. It is the custom from ancient days that students can give any dakshina or offering to the teacher. It's an old custom, and still the custom exists because teachers don't have any specific money or income. What the disciples give from their hearts, the teachers use for their own help, or for helping humanity. Students can offer anything: fruits, flowers, money, garland, anything. Whatever they have. They always give whatever they can to contribute to the welfare of the teacher and his organization and so on. That is allowed.

But you cannot sell mantra or demand, "I want such and such things for my mantra." This demand cannot be made by the teacher. It is against all spiritual growth. No mantra can be sold, nor can a mantra be concocted, nor are there any new mantras. There are specific mantras that exist and there are no new mantras. We can not create nor can we give a different mantra to every individual. It is not possible; no one can do it and call themselves spiritual gurus.

It is often asked, "Must we keep our mantras secret?" You must keep it secret, but that means just not exposing it to everybody. If I am going to chant my mantra, I'm not going to tell everybody, "I'm going to repeat!" If someone wants to know, and there's a purpose behind the curiosity, you can tell; there's no harm, you see. That's all. That's the only secret.

So what do you do after mantra initiation? Initiation alone is not sufficient. Initiation is just like igniting the fire. We are only using one small match stick to light the fire, is it not? Well, suppose you ignited a fire with a small match stick, but you don't have kindling wood and papers, what will happen? It will go out. The match stick, the initiation, has no value then. Immediately, after lighting the fire, you have to add more paper and more fuel to make more fire, to make it bigger and bigger and bigger. You make the fire huge. Then it will give you enough strength and energy; it won't go out easily.

The more times you repeat the more the fire grows, bigger and bigger. Then there will come a level, a very high level, you are almost meditating on the transcendental level. At that level your mind automatically enters meditation. The moment you start *Om Namah Sivaya* your mind goes directly and you are meditating on the higher level. There's no sound in any form, not vocal form or telepathic form. It's only in the transcendental state, the sound vibrates. The vibration of *Om Namah Sivaya, Om Namah Sivaya* goes on intensely. The power of that energy is now vibrating at a very high level; that's called meditation.

You start as beginners, *Om Namah Sivaya, Om Namah Sivaya.* You start verbally, then you go to mental repetition. Mental is more powerful than verbal. Eventually you stop even mental repetition and you enter the telepathic level where the sound and the name merge in a telepathic state. Then you transcend that and come to the invisible energy state where you become one with the form you are meditating on. You and Siva, or you and Krishna, become one and the same. There's no difference in that last state; the meditator and the meditated are one and the same. You become the object of the meditation just like your mind takes the shape of an orange to see the orange, so you become Krishna to see Krishna, or become Siva. But they are not different deities; Siva is not different from Krishna; nor is Krishna different from Rama nor is Rama different from Devi or Goddess. They are all one and the same. According to your relationship or temperament, one is more easy to approach and to meditate on.

Repeat the mantra after getting the initiation. Don't just drop it. You must meditate regularly. You got it everybody?

Swamiji gave mantra initiation to anyone who asked for it. There is no record of how many people he personally initiated, but it must be in the thousands. He believed that mantra initiation was the necessary first step along the road to God Realization, and was always willing to help anyone who wanted to take that first step. In conjunction with mantra initiation he would also give you a spiritual name if you wanted one. This name was the name of a Hindu deity, an aspect of God, usually related to your mantra. It was something to live up to. If your name was a name for God, you came closer to becoming God. Every time you addressed another person in the organization, you spoke to God. In this way Swamiji encouraged us to see God in ourselves and in everyone else.

Mantra initiation had a profound effect on many people. It was a symbolic transition from one life to another, from a worldly life to a life of the spirit.

Swamiji gives a student mantra initiation.

It was March, 1978, at the yoga retreat in Nassau. As our Teachers Training Course neared its conclusion, it was announced that Swamiji would be giving mantra initiation for those students who were interested. I decided not to participate in this as I had learned over the month that often when I came into direct contact with Swamiji events took a turn different from what I had anticipated. The course had given me a tremendous amount to mull over already and I didn't feel ready to get in any deeper.

Mantra initiation came and went and now it was the afternoon on which Swamiji was leaving for India. We had some free time. I had decided to do some reading and to get some sun and was sitting in bathing suit and shorts on the bay platform, leaning against the low wall of the temple.

A few people dressed all in white, carrying fruits and flowers, came in and sat down in the temple behind me. A few minutes later Swamiji entered and began to pray. I figured this ceremony must have something do with his leave-taking, and asked a staff member passing by what the meaning of it was.

He explained that Swamiji was giving mantra initiation again, for those students who had been unable to attend the first time or had decided belatedly that they wanted this. Swamiji was to leave for the airport immediately following, in twenty minutes. I thought, "Good. Now I can watch for myself what goes on and decide whether to take this step later on."

So I half-turned and sat looking over the wall, listening to Swamiji's prayers. Then the first two of the aspirants came forward and sat right at his feet. He began repetition of their chosen mantra, Om Namah Sivaya.

Mentally, I was drawn right into it the second he started. My breath started going with it, in rhythm, and I seemed to be hearing it both outside and inside my head at the same time in a very powerful and concrete way. Although all throughout the course I had used OM in my meditations, and had not chosen a mantra, I now thought, "Well, this must be my mantra."

Then, a second later, "And this must be my mantra initiation!"

Although Swamiji went on to initiate several other aspirants in several other mantras, I continued to hear only Om Namah Sivaya. Before I realized it was over, Swamiji suddenly got up and left the temple, exiting by the wooden door just a few feet from where I was sitting in my bathing suit, leaning against the wall. He paused for just a second and looked directly at me and smiled. I must have looked totally stunned.

Five minutes later a large crowd began to gather on the platform to see Swamiji off. I walked back to my tent, zipped it all up and sat in it.

Madalasa
Ottawa, Ontario, Canada

ॐ नमो नारायणाय

In the early 1980's, I was operating my own law office in Century City, California, specializing in entertainment law. The stress and frustration of it was starting literally to kill me; I was becoming a nervous wreck. I knew I had to do something.

Through a series of friends and referrals, I started doing hatha yoga at the Sivananda Yoga Center on Sunset Boulevard. I experienced relief immediately, and knew I had come "home."

Shortly after I started going to the center, they announced that Swami Vishnu was coming for a visit, and would give a talk. I decided to see what he was about, and went to the lecture. After he finished they announced that Swami Vishnu would be giving mantra initiation for all who wished to stay. "Why not?" I thought, "Perhaps another interesting experience; certainly something much different from lawyering."

All the people who stayed after Swamiji's talk selected the mantra they would receive, and divided into groups. Swamiji worked with each group separately, going over the exact words of the mantra until the vibrations were said correctly, or so it seemed.

Then it was the turn of the Lakshmi mantra group, which I had selected. We sat around Swamiji on the floor in the center of the meditation room, and repeated the mantra with Swamiji until we all got it right. It was electrifying on a level I did not then understand. It was intimidating to look into Swamiji's eyes, to make even minimal contact with him. There was so much power and force there. It was all so new and unknown.

After everybody in the group got it correctly (or said it, or felt it or whatever; who can know on how many levels Swamiji was teaching?), Swamiji sent us off to a corner to repeat the mantra 108 times. As I repeated my new mantra, I knew something was different, but it was impossible to know then what it was.

That night I did not sleep one wink, not one minute. I seemed to be vibrating (literally vibrating, like tingling) with some kind of strange, new energy. It was not scary or frightening. It was energizing and new. When dawn finally came I went about my business that day, not tired and fatigued, but filled with something exciting, a vibration and energy so different from the miserable energy from my law practice, it gave me a new sense of joy and hope I had not had before. It was the beginning of the most profound changes in my life.

Larry Allman
Los Angeles, California

ॐ नमो नारायणाय

One summer at the Yoga Camp in Val Morin I decided to ask Swami Vishnu about a mantra I was using. A few years before I had been involved with another *guru*, but I broke with him. While I was now fully committed to Swamiji and the Sivananda Yoga organization I was still using the mantra given to me by my first teacher.

Swamiji suggested that I choose a new mantra. After pondering a number of mantras I narrowed the choice down to two. Being unable to decide further I approached Swamiji. He asked a few questions and, because I was a yoga teacher, Swamiji said that I should use one of the two and that he would initiate me into the mantra.

At the appointed time I was ushered into Swamiji's house and taken to Swamiji's own meditation room. What a surprise and an honor! I entered and offered Swamiji the flowers and fruit that I had brought. He told me I shouldn't give these gifts to him but rather I should offer them to God and Swami Sivananda. I was struck by the difference between Swamiji who wanted nothing, not even the symbolic fruits and flowers, and my first spiritual teacher who insisted on receiving $350 for mantra initiation.

I placed the offerings on the altar and sat in front of Swamiji. What happened is truly indescribable. My body dissolved. My mind seemed to expand infinitely. My consciousness changed and instead of being aware of forms and colors, I became aware of pure knowledge. The knowledge did not accumulate as in daily living. It was simply there, presented to me whole and resplendent.

To the casual outside observer, all that would have been apparent was Swamiji repeating the mantra, then asking me to repeat the mantra, at first with him and then by myself. This did occur, but what really happened was that Swamiji used his power to take my mind and energy, lift and shape them, and elevate them to the highest degree possible. I was introduced to and submerged in the full power of the mantra and had the power instilled in my psyche. This was a truly transcendental experience and one that I had been seeking.

Then Swamiji released his power and my vision began to fade because I didn't have the ability to maintain that realm of Truth. I felt a twinge of regret that the experience was fading and for a moment thought I was losing it. Then I realized I had lost nothing. What Swamiji had done was to activate the power of the mantra in me. My job was to repeat the mantra enough so that my mind would return to that state and access the power of the mantra directly, this time through my own efforts.

Swamiji had initiated me into the power and mystery of the mantra. He had given me the tools and confidence to access that power and mystery directly. He had also given me faith. Through this initiation, Swamiji had demonstrated to me the literal truth of the Vedanta teachings. There were no more doubts.

Shankara
Ottawa, ON, Canada

ॐ नमो नारायणाय

Tomorrow Swami Vishnu would be 50 years old. A huge dinner and celebration was planned. Today he was giving out mantras, investing them, and I was to get mine. We were standing in a long shivering line, knee deep in snow. We'd been fasting since yesterday. I was hungry, cold, grouchy. Most people had fruits in their hands, gifts for Swamiji, but I had a small plastic bag of lumpy cookies my children had made. I wanted to give him a meaningful gift, a gift from my heart. And I was missing my children.

Phil, my boyfriend and yoga teacher, stood with me in line. He was telling me how wonderful it would be when I got my mantra, how something magical would happen. How high I'd be, how happy. I've always been half cynic and half believer. Half of me thought this whole mantra business was ridiculous. The other half was excited, hopeful and a little afraid. Phil was showing me a list of mantras in a yoga pamphlet. There was one particular mantra that drew me, but Phil thought I should take a different one. I couldn't decide which mantra to choose. The line was rapidly getting shorter and shorter, and I just couldn't decide.

Then I was alone with Swamiji. He asked me which mantra I'd chosen. I said it. He signaled for me to kneel. He repeated the mantra, passing his hand over my head and the mantra came alive, settled into my heart, and began speaking itself. The sound of it made me feel sick. I stuck the bag of cookies into his hand, staggered out of that room, nauseous, gagging. "How was it?" asked Phil, smiling his wide expectant smile. I couldn't even answer.

That night I couldn't eat supper. I couldn't sleep with Phil. All night I huddled in the dry bathtub of our cabin, sobbing, vomiting. The mantra was like a sickness, like an unwanted pregnancy. It had lodged itself in my chest, a fat black slug stuck to my heart, and it wouldn't stop speaking itself.

Morning came, New Years Eve day, and then lunch time, time for Swamiji's birthday feast. The dining hall was packed with people from all over the world, smiling in all sorts of languages, everyone smiling. We kneeled or sat on pillows at the long, long dining table. Swamiji was seated at the head of the table, all smiles. Only I wasn't smiling. I was so sick I could hardly breath. I couldn't even try to taste my food.

Then it was like I was watching myself, standing up, stumbling along the edge of the table, over peoples arms, over their heads, their babies. "Excuse me... Excuse me... Excuse me..." Until I was there at the head of the table beside Swamiji. "Please," I begged, "I have to see you." He told me to come to his cabin at two o'clock.

At two I was there at his cabin. He had other guests, a family from India, mother, father, son. What I remember is this: As I came to the door Swamiji was telling the boy that his name was a Sanskrit word meaning "discrimination" and that this was a very significant name. He should consider its meaning. As he was speaking Swami Vishnu was walking around the room serving from a small tray the cookies my children had made. The guests were eating the cookies, saying how good they were.

Then the guest left and I was alone with him. "Well?" he asked me. "It's the mantra," I stammered. "I picked the wrong mantra. Please, I need a new mantra."

Swamiji kind of chuckled. "You don't need a new mantra," he said. "The mantra doesn't have a problem. You have a problem. Come over here." So I came close and he had me kneel down in front of him. Then he murmured some words in Sanskrit, passing his hand over my head. As he did that I felt powerful waves surging through me, through my whole being. When I stood up I was dizzy with happiness.

In a way nothing had changed. The mantra was still there, stronger than ever, repeating and repeating itself in my heart, but instead of feeling like a parasite it felt warm, like love, pulsing inside me. Later when I met Phil on the path by the Krishna temple the smile I gave him was huge. "You see?" he told me.

The mantra never did stop, never ran down, so that now, 15 years later, almost a decade since I've seen Phil, five years since my own father died, one year since my youngest child left home, six months since Swamiji died, it remains the one thing I can count on.

Joan Dobbie
Eugene, Oregon

ॐ नमो नारायणाय

I received mantra initiation in 1978 at the Yoga Ranch in Woodbourne. I can still feel the touch of his finger on my forehead.

Charlene Gordon
Victoria, British Columbia

Just One More Story

Swamiji was a master storyteller, with a seemingly endless repertoire. In evening satsang he would often talk about complex philosophical ideas. To make sure we got the point he would reinforce his talk with a story. By this time he may have been talking for and hour or more, it would be late, people would be tired. He would always say, "Just one more story..." We would always laugh, knowing that one more story might turn into two or three. We didn't care. It was like being a child, and hearing stories before going to sleep. You didn't even have to ask for more so you could stay up a bit later; Swamiji would always be glad to oblige. Here is one of his favorites.

This story is about a shepherd and his sheep living in a valley. One night a pregnant mountain lioness came to hunt amongst the sheep. When the shepherd saw the mountain lion he started shooting at her. The shooting frightened her. Suddenly she gave birth to her lion cub, and then ran away to the forest, leaving her cub among the sheep. Luckily there was a nursing sheep. She started nursing the new born lion cub. So the lion cub started thinking that the sheep was his mother, and he started to bleat like sheep - Baa Baa Baa Baa. He was drinking milk and eating grass, becoming a vegetarian. So the lion cub grew up among the sheep thinking that he is just like any other sheep.

After several years, the king of the forest, a big mountain lion, came to the sheep's valley to hunt. There he saw among the sheep one of his own royal family members, bleating like a sheep, eating grass. What a disgrace! It was like Prince Charles going to live with the hippies. What would Queen Elizabeth think? That's what the lion king thought. "What a disgrace to our royal family!"

So he ran shouting at the sheeplion, "What are you doing with the sheep? Why you are bleating like a sheep?"

And the sheeplion was terrified. Seeing the mountain lion running after him, he shouted, "Mommy! Mommy help me! This fellow is going to kill me!"

But the sheep mother ran away and the mountain lion caught the sheeplion. "Don't be afraid of me. You are a lion like me."

"Oh no no! I'm not a lion. I'm a sheep. I've got my mommy there, my beautiful mommy. "Mommy! Let me go to my mommy!"

"Oh no! You are not a sheep. You are a lion like me."

"Please leave me alone. I beg you lion, let me go."

"No. No. No. I'm going to take you and show you who you are." So he dragged him to the mountain against his will and brought him to a big lake, "Look in that lake. What do you see?"

His eyes shut tight. "No. No, I don't want to open my eyes. I am afraid."

"Don't be afraid. Just look. See who you are."

"I know who I am. I'm a sheep. I got my mommy; I got three brothers and two sisters; I live in the valley."

"Oh no, that's all wrong. Look! You have forgotten who you are." After some time, the sheeplion opened his eyes. "What do you see?"

"I see waves."

"Wait for the waves to subside." After some time there were no more waves, no more ripples; the lake was as smooth as glass. Suddenly he saw his face. He didn't look like a sheep. He saw the other lion's face beside his. "Hey I am like you. You are like me. I am you. You are me. We are both kings!"

And the mountain lion said, "Don't bleat like a sheep. Roar like a lion! Go to your kingdom in the forest and enjoy your life."

So for the first time in his life, he roared. No more bleating like a sheep. He realized who he was and lived happily ever after in the forest, in his kingdom.

Who are the sheeplions of this story? We all are. We are bleating morning till evening: Baa Baa Baa I am German, Baa Baa Baa East German, Baa Baa Baa West German, Baa Baa Baa I'm Russian, Baa Baa Baa American, Baa Baa Baa Protestant, Baa Baa Baa Catholic, Baa Baa Baa I'm a Jew, Baa Baa Baa I'm Arab, Baa Baa Baa I'm a PLO, Baa Baa Baa I'm Chancellor, Baa Baa Baa Prime Minister, Baa Baa Baa I am male, Baa Baa Baa I'm female, Baa Baa Baa I am a Swami, Baa Baa Baa. That's all we are doing all day long.

The mountain lions, the great masters, like Jesus and Sivananda, come and say, "Oh, you are bleating like a sheep. You are not a German, an Austrian, Russian or American. You are the immortal self. I am in you. You are in me. I am He. I am Brahman. You too are Brahman. You too are God. But this body is not God. Look within. You'll find who you are." "Oh no, no! I don't want to find out who I am. I know who I am. I am a Swami. I have three ashrams; I have ten students. I have two hundred and twenty rooms and thirty bathrooms. I have money, two million dollars in the bank. Master says, "Hey, that's not you. These things just belong to you." "Oh no, no! I have my wife and children." "They won't come with you. They're all objects." "Oh no, no, no! I love my wife and children very much; I have a beautiful home and a lovely family, children." And the teacher says, "Don't bleat like a sheep. When you die will your wife go with you? Will your children go with you? Can you take all your money with you?" He starts thinking, "Hey, something is wrong here."

You will also die. You can't take your credit card with you. You can't even take this body with you. The germs are waiting for it. Death is waiting for you because you identify with this body. You are immortal. "Oh Teacher, tell me how to find it, how to escape death." "I'll show you come with me."

Close your eyes. Look within, in that mind-lake. What do you see? Pizza, ice cream, bananas; heart beating, lungs breathing. They're all objects. That's not you. You are not a heart, or lungs, etc. Just close you eyes and breathe very gently. Practice. Go on, practice. You must practice breathing gently every day. When there are no more thought waves, what do you see? Now Teacher, I am you. You are me. There is neither disciple nor teacher, neither I nor God; we are one. I am in everything; everything is in me. I am that I am. Aham Brahma Asmi. Sohum. I am He. I am He. Sohum.

Swamiji was always trying to make us look beyond our limited view of ourselves and the world. Sometimes fiercely, sometimes gently, always with great love, he made us open our minds. No matter how we resisted, he helped us slowly change, to let go of our models of how things were or should be and to see our true Selves.

When Swamiji spoke, I generally listened with rapt attention because he seemed to be giving words to intrinsic truths, the sorts of things I longed to hear but about which no one ever spoke. Swamiji had one theme however, which left me very uneasy. He would sometimes speak about the different roles of men and women in society. He saw these roles as being psychologically determined and attributed a lot of unhappiness in family life to people's attempts to disregard these "natural" roles. I felt that here he was speaking from a certain culturally-conditioned perspective and not from the perspective of any universal truth. I never confronted him about it. People usually did not argue with Swamiji.

One day during his discourse, Swamiji again came around to this theme. Whereas his words on all other subjects aroused feelings of joy, I could feel my anger rising up strongly as he began again to give his views on the essentially different psychology of men and women. Before I had time to think about it, I had burst out to the effect that, although I usually felt the righteousness and truth in Swamiji's words, on this matter, I could not. I tried to go barreling on to explain about cultural perspectives, historical needs, etc. but Swamiji quickly cut me off.

"Madalasa", he bellowed. "Are you a Jew or a Christian?" I was caught off guard, but tried to answer thoughtfully, "Well, both. Or neither. I was born to a Jewish family and brought up in that religion, but later I learned to appreciate the truths of Jesus' teachings and his greatness. On the other hand, other religions also teach the same truths, so I don't *feel* now that I am particularly a Jew or a Christian."

Swamiji nodded curtly. He already knew this about me. He immediately proceeded, still quite loudly. "Are you an American or a Canadian?"

"Well, Swamiji, I was born an American. My family is in America, but I moved to Canada over ten years ago now and have Canadian citizenship. I'm not a very political or a very patriotic person and I don't really *feel* like either an American or a Canadian. I guess I'm sort of a world-citizen."

Again, he nodded curtly and then inquired, "Are you a man or a woman?"

This question required no thought. Immediately I replied, "Well, of course, Swamiji, I'm a woman."

He said nothing, just sat back with a big smile and waited for my own stupidity to dawn on me. I was aware from his silence and his expression that I had just fallen right into some monumental trap but I couldn't see it. I just felt confused.

After a moment's silence he chided me, "You do not identify with race, religion or nationality. You know that these are accidents of birth. You identify with the Immortal Self which remains unchanged. So, if I make jokes about Jews or Hindus, or Catholics priests or American presidents, you are never upset. (This was true, I reflected.) But whenever the subject of men and women comes up, you have a strong emotional reaction and lose all discrimination. You cannot listen. This is because you are identifying with this role. You are not a woman, anymore than you are a Jew, a Buddhist, a German, a Canadian. These bodies too are just like clothes that we put on, only to discard them when they wear out. You have been a woman, as well as a man, thousands of times. Remember this, identify with your true Self, the Immortal Atman, and don't be so easily upset!"

Madalasa
Ottawa, Ontario, Canada

For some of Swamiji's students, the ultimate step in the process of their spiritual growth was taking vows of *sanyas*. Swamiji was a monk in the Saraswati order of sanyas which goes back in an unbroken lineage to Sankaracharya, the 8th century philosopher-saint. One of the duties of a *sanyasin* is to initiate others into the order.

When someone takes the vows of *sanyas,* they literally give up their previous life. They take a new name, and are never referred to by their old name. They are no longer that body, that ego. That identity is symbolically cast into the fire during the sanyas ceremony. They identify only with the true Self, the unchanging Atman. *Sanyasins* wears orange, the color of fire, to constantly remind them of their act of renunciation.

Swamiji gave over 100 students *sanyas,* starting in the early 1960's and ending with Swami Jahardhananda, who took *sanyas* in the summer of 1993, only a few months before Swamiji's death. There were approximately equal numbers of men and women who took *sanyas* from Swamiji.

Were all these people perfect saints? Did they all really have no identification with the body? Of course not. Swamiji saw the taking of sanyas as a step along the road. The vows were a shield and armor to protect the aspirant in his or her struggle. Swamiji had the same attitude as his teacher Sivananda, who even gave people sanyas by mail!

Generally, to become a swami takes several years. In the past one sometime had to stay six or seven or eight years with the master before you would be initiated as a swami. Some masters are very strict to see whether the student has the strength to become a swami. But Master Swami Sivananda had a different idea. He thought that most of the young people who came to him had *sanyas samskaras,* impressions from previous lives as swamis, but were afraid to go ahead, thinking they may not have the strength .

Actually nobody is perfect enough to become a pure swami; it's not possible in one life to become a completely pure swami, to follow every strict rule. In one life, it is not possible. So, Master thought that even if someone may not be able to be a one hundred percent swami, if he can only be a twenty percent swami, it is much better than to be no swami at all. So that's what he did. His ideas were quite different from all of ours. The other swamis didn't like it; the other gurus didn't like it. They complained, "Swami Sivananda initiates everyone into the swami order and that's not the right thing, you know. One needs special qualifications."

Master's idea was that it is better to aim at a lion, and miss him, than to aim at a jackal and catch it. Anyone can catch a jackal, but to catch a lion, one must be strong. Everyone should aim high. Even if the result was failure, it's much better. So that was Master's idea. In one life, someone may not be able to be a one hundred percent swami. But even twenty percent in this life is something, next life he'll be another forty, up to sixty percent, so he's getting closer isn't he?

Swamiji was also always very understanding when people decided that the life of the sanyasin was no longer for them.

When I renounced my vows of sanyas I was hesitant because I thought that Swamiji would really try and coax me to stay and not go. To my surprise he was very loving and understanding. What he told me was that names and forms and titles don't mean anything. The most important thing in life is to do your sadhana. If you do your sadhana, everything else will take care of itself.

At that moment in place of Swamiji I saw my father, who had died two years before. He looked at me and smiled. Then again it was Swamiji smiling at me. I gave him a big hug. I realized that I would always do my sadhana and that Swamiji would always be my spiritual teacher and guide, my spiritual father.

Neelakanta
Washington, D.C.

Many of Swamiji's stories illustrated points from the classical teachings of vedanta and raja yoga philosophy. One favorite was the Heaven and Hell Story. This version was told while he was sitting in a parking lot in India with a number of students, waiting for two buses to come. The buses were, as usual, late.

Sitting here, in this parking lot, is heaven or hell depending on your state of mind. If your mind is happy, you can sit very comfortably in the shade of the tree and meditate. If your mind is unhappy, you can be sitting in a palace but it will make no difference, it will all be dross. Heaven and hell are only in the mind. I'll tell you a small story.

So many people heard about heaven and hell. They wanted to see how people live in these places. Heaven and hell, you know, are neighbors; there is just a big wall in between, heaven on one side and hell on the other. So those people went for a tour.

They went to hell first. All the people there were having food, laid out on a big table. But their arms were held straight by long wooden spoons tied to them, making it impossible to bend at the elbows. They had to eat by throwing the food up in the air and catching it in their mouths. The food was going everywhere, with now and then a small piece falling into their mouths.

The people on tour then went to the other side of the wall, to heaven. Here everything was the same, except these people had gold plates and long golden spoons were tied to their arms. Here, however, everyone was enjoying their food, because they were picking up food in their spoons and serving each other.

Heaven and hell aren't places up in the sky and down under the earth. They are always right here, right now. We make our own heaven and hell by the state of our mind. It is up to us. We can control the mind, and be in heaven, or let the mind 'run wild like a monkey' as Swamiji used to say, and be in hell. We can think only of ourselves, and be miserable, or spend our lives serving others, and be happy. All actions are preceded by thoughts. We can choose which thoughts to follow through on, which actions to take. If we learn to control our thoughts, to have only positive uplifting thoughts, life will be heaven on earth.

Some people who came in contact with Swamiji weren't ready for his teachings, couldn't absorb what he was saying. They were so wrapped up in their own mental hell that he couldn't reach them directly. He tried to help them all the same.

Once a middle-aged woman came and asked me for some help. I asked what I could do for her.

She said, "Only you can help me, Swamiji."

"What's the problem?"

"First off, I can't sleep. Secondly, a priest is controlling me."

"Why can't you sleep?"

"The air conditioning is making noise in my room so I can't sleep."

"Turn off the air conditioning. You don't need my help," I intellectually explained. "Why are you using air conditioning? You are living in the mountains."

"Some say it is good for my arthritis, so I use the air conditioning."

So I told her the cool air would make her pain worse. She needed more warmth, "Shut it off, then you'll be able to sleep."

But she said, "No, I paid $1,000 for it and the salesman said it would help me."

She continued arguing in her own way and I knew there was no use of approaching her intellectually. I had already explained everything intellectually to her: 1) the air conditioning is bad for her arthritis and 2) she doesn't need air conditioning here in the mountains. But she knows that she paid $1,000 for her air conditioning, and the salesman told her that it would help her. So now, she cannot get free of that suggestion he made to her.

I know there is no way I can approach her intellectually, as I already tried, so, I simply told her that I would help her. I told her to come again and I would give her some special breathing and mantras, and special meditation and relaxation techniques so that she could go to sleep. She thought I was going to do some kind of magic things because I came from India, from the Himalayas. She thought I must have some kind of powers, more so than the salesman.

Her second problem was the priest. She said she went to him, and she talked to him, and now he was controlling her all the time. She wanted to get out of his control. I said I would help her with that problem also. With that, the conversation was closed and the meeting was over.

Ten days later, I was giving a private class when my secretary called from the center. She said that a very agitated lady wanted to speak to me. The lady said that I had given her some treatment and that she wanted to talk to me about it. I took the call.

The first thing she said was, "Swamiji, I don't want your treatment anymore."

I was shocked. I didn't know who the person was; she never introduced herself. I asked, "Who are you? What is your name?"

She said that she was the person who came and saw me in the camp, the one who needed help with sleeping, and the priest. Now, she didn't want my treatment anymore. I knew immediately that there was no use explaining intellectually. I had never given her any treatment. I had merely told her, "Come here. I'll teach you a little *asanas,* a little *pranayama,* etc. Through all this you'll be able to relax. And I'll help you from the priest by praying for you." That's all I had said.

I did not understand at the time I "treated her" what I had done to her. Her mind was like putty. It changed into the shape of anyone with whom she came into contact. A salesman came and gave her the idea that without air conditioning she wouldn't feel well. So, she took that advice. And then a priest said, "You must do this, and your sin will go away." So, she got into that. She came to a Swami because she wanted to get over a priest, and when I said I was going to help her, her mind came under my influence. I did not know this until then. So now she still felt that I was controlling her. She did not know any other person to go to. If she could have found some other higher authority, she would have gone there.

The minute I realized her mental condition, I knew how to approach her. I simply said, "From this moment onward, I take back all my treatment."

She was so happy. From that time onwards there was no problem from the sleepless nights, from the priest, or from me either.

Many people who came in touch with Swamiji learned to see more clearly how their minds operated. Through the understanding that this knowledge gave them, they grew and their lives became a little more heavenly.

I first met Swamiji at teacher training in Vigo, Spain in 1986. A short, dynamic, funny, tender man, he made a strong impression fast. Looking back I realize I was lucky to have had the first hand experience of Swamiji as my teacher. He was intense and demanding. He pushed and cajoled us, made us stay up late at night while he tried to get his message across. Most of all I think he wanted us to wake up and realize our Selves and our responsibilities to life.

One of the greatest lessons I learned was going beyond self-made boundaries. Often Swamiji would push us to our limits and beyond. This would bring up incredible resistance in me as I hate being pressured and pushed.

However, by getting past this negativity and just getting on with things I found I could achieve more than I ever dreamed. The power of positive (and negative!) thinking became very clear.

Shanti
Vancouver, British Columbia

ॐ नमो नारायणाय

Swamiji taught me many lessons the summer I took advanced teacher training. One time I got very angry with someone else taking the course and was ready to really tell them off. That evening at *satsang* I had a very strong vision. I actually saw and felt that the same light shining in Swamiji was shining in me and everyone else, including that other person. It was a very strong experience. My anger completely subsided and in its place was compassion and awe.

Amba
Val Morin, Quebec

Learning Through Serving

Swamiji's *guru*, Swami Sivananda, placed great stress on karma yoga, the yoga of selfless service of humanity. He taught that it was the best way to soften your heart and remove your negative qualities. Swamiji learned many important lessons by watching how Sivananda used karma yoga to help people grow spiritually.

A woman from Bombay wrote a letter to Master saying, "I want to arrange a benefit performance, a special Indian dance, to collect money for Sivananda *Ashram*, Master's *Ashram* at Rishikesh. Shall I do this program for you and collect money in Bombay and send it to you? I want your blessing, and your advice and permission."

Master got this letter, looked at it and called me, "Vishnu Swamiji, call Param Swamiji here."

Now Param Swamiji was the senior disciple, the first swami who came to Master when Master was still in Swargashram doing his early penance.

We called Paramanandaji from his office. Master handed him the letter. "Paramanandaji, please reply to this letter. It is about a benefit performance."

Swami Paramanandaji is a little bit of a business-minded Swami. Master had no idea of this type of thing; who is good at doing business and who is cunning, who can be trusted, etc. So he gave the letter to Paramanandaji who just looked at it. He knew this lady very well. She was not really a person you could trust. She might collect money in Master's name and not even send it to him, or she may send a little and keep the rest, and there would be no way to know which she would do. So, what should he do? She had been to the *ashram* several times and Master knew Paramananda didn't like her.

See Master's beauty? Master knew that Paramanandaji didn't like this lady. So when her letter came he gave it to him. There were so many other swamis he could have given the letter to, but he wouldn't give it to anyone else. He called Paramanandaji and said, "You reply to this letter." And that's all. He wouldn't say anything else.

Paramanandaji took this letter with some others and went to his office and read it. He answered the letter with the words, "My blessings are with you; go ahead and do this performance,." But he knew that she might not actually be honest in dealing with our *ashram.* So he shouldn't say yes. Suppose he said no; suppose he said "Please cancel this program. Don't do it; it is not necessary at this moment." But if he wrote that, Master might think that Paramanandaji doesn't like her. So, what to do? He is in a dilemma: if he says yes it is bad; if he says no it is also bad.

So he wrote two small cards. One card said, "My blessings are with you; please carry on this function." The other card said, "I don't think so; this is not the time." He typed both cards—one yes card and one no card—and brought them to Master for his signature. He left them on Master's table to let him choose which one he wanted. That way the blame will not come on him.

So what did Master do? He saw Paramanandaji and looked at both cards. He took his pen, signed both cards, and gave them back to Paramanandaji and asked, "Are you going to send both cards?"

So that is the way Master tested the students and found out their reactions. Each one of us has a different temperament and mentality and spiritual evolution and strength. All are not equal when they go to Master. And Master had to take care of them. Life is not easy. Now I can go back and see. At that time I couldn't realize how much struggle and trouble he had to undergo because I was only a teenager. Most of the people there, like Paramanandaji, etc., were grown-up people and Master had to adapt and adjust and accommodate with all these type of students. It is not an easy thing. Now I can see it; not at that time. Now I myself undergo all those problems.

Swamiji always placed great stress on the value of selfless service. He said that there was no way you could just meditate and do asanas all day long, you needed other things to fill your time usefully. He often told the story of how he had gone away from Sivananda's ashram, to meditate alone in the wilderness, sitting by the Ganges. After a few days of intense meditation he became restless. He couldn't meditate all day long, and ended up spending hours skipping stones across a pool of water, just to fill in the time. He quickly realized that what he needed was something useful to do with his time, and returned to the ashram and a life of active service. Like his *guru* before him, Swamiji made service one of the cornerstones of his teaching.

Anyone could do service. You could do it anywhere, at any time. There are countless opportunities to serve others. Not only the action itself was important but the state of mind as you performed the act was also significant. You had to learn to serve others without any expectations of reward, without desire for the fruits of your actions. Just do the work to the best of your abilities, feeling that every act is an act of worship.

Swamiji would often ask you to do something that on the surface, from your limited viewpoint, seemed like a bad idea. It was best not to argue; he always had his reasons, much more important than ours.

> Before coming to the yoga retreat in Nassau my background was boating. Thus I was given the responsibility of taking care of the boats. One day Swamiji told us that the *Ananda Kutir*, one of the house boats, should be hauled (taken out of the water at the marina) and that the bottom should be done: cleaned, necessary repairs carried out, and the bottom painted with an anti-fouling marine paint.
>
> I thought this was a waste of time and money because this boat's hull was made of fiberglass so there was nothing that could be hurt by its sitting in the water for a long time. Furthermore, it wasn't necessary to clean the bottom because removal of marine growth from the bottom of a boat is usually done to allow the boat to move more easily through the water. This boat never went anywhere; it was permanently moored at our dock. I was experienced in these matters. I knew what was a waste of money and time and what wasn't.
>
> But Swamiji insisted. The more I argued, the more adamant he was that this boat should be hauled.
>
> And it was hauled. What we found was something no one, no matter how much marine experience he had, could have predicted.
>
> After it was out of the water we saw that years before a previous owner had bolted onto the fiberglass hull a long wooden keel in order to make the boat maneuver better while under power. Over the years the keel had been badly eaten away by marine worms and the bolts that held the keel to the hull were almost loose. In another year or so the bolts would have become loose, allowing the keel to drop a bit, thus allowing water to come into the hull through the bolt holes. The boat would have sunk.
>
> Obviously, Swamiji had no way of knowing this experientially or intellectually. He was operating from a higher intuitive plane, showing us how we have to follow that inner voice.
>
> Bharata
> Nassau, Bahamas

ॐ नमो नारायणाय

> Sometime around 1985, after I had taken the teachers' training course, I was at the farm in Grass Valley, California, where Swami Vishnuji was giving a program. I had worked on some prior legal matters with him for the organization, so he had gotten to know me a little. He used to say that lawyers had some of the strangest *karma* to work through. I think he gave me a little bit of special attention just because I was a lawyer, and he knew I was trying to live a more spiritual life while at the same time walking through the cesspools, lies, etc., which lawyers seem to necessarily traverse as a profession. He had really

mystical knowledge about how strange it is to be a lawyer in any kind of spiritual context.

During the course of his program at the farm, he pulled me aside so that he, I, and the farm's director could have a meeting concerning the farm and a point of real estate law. The farm's main 40-acre parcel and the 20-acre parcel containing Swamiji's house and the Durga Temple were separated by a neighbor's 20 acre parcel. For years students had walked over the neighbor's parcel. There was even a well worn path.

Swamiji asked me to protect the organization's rights for the students to walk across the neighbor's property, based on having done so for over ten years without protest or obstruction. When I told him it was not possible without actually formally purchasing those rights from the owner and recording a document with the county recorder, he told me I was wrong, and instructed that I look into it. I would never argue with Swamiji, but I knew I was right.

My research revealed an obscure line of California cases which provided exactly what Swamiji thought was possible, an Easement By Prescription. He was basically right, and I was basically wrong. However in this type of Easement, the law required the payment of taxes for the past 5 years, and the filing of a lawsuit to perfect these rights as a matter of public record.

I sent a written report of my findings to Swamiji in which I took the position that it would not be advisable to pursue this easement because of the impact such a lawsuit would have on the local people in Grass Valley towards the Farm. Swamiji sent back word to me that he agreed with my advice 100%. In all my dealings with Swamiji after this incident, I perceived that Swamiji felt comfortable trusting me and my judgment on things. I had somehow earned his respect. And from this incident onward, I knew that Swamiji possessed some really superior knowledge, some tremendously mystical understanding of things that we mortals could never fully comprehend. How else could a spiritual man from India have specific knowledge about Easements By Prescription in California?

Larry Allman
Los Angeles, CA

Practicing *karma* yoga meant that you also had to surrender to the *guru,* since he would often ask you to do things that you might not ordinarily want to do or enjoy doing.

After having spent six months on staff at the Yoga Camp in Val Morin, I was transferred to the London Centre. The day before I left, a beautiful and long *satsang* was going on and I was feeling a little sad, because I thought that I wouldn't see Swamiji anymore. Swamiji was very ill and withdrawing more and more. At that time, a staff was needed who could take care of him. I wanted to suggest to Swamiji that I stay in Canada and serve him.

After the *satsang* I was hesitant to ask him because there were so many people around him. I tried to shout "Swamiji" but no one heard me. I was even a bit jealous of all the swamis and people around him, because no one else was able to come close to him. The wheelchair had already been turned towards the exit.

Just when I was feeling that I was nobody and nothing and that it would not be possible for me to ask Swamiji even a single question, he asked Swami Kartikeyananda to push his wheelchair back towards the hall and asked "What does Sadasiva want?" My whole body was shaken for a moment. "He is speaking to me!" I was thinking. Then I asked, "Can I stay with you and serve you?"

Swamiji answered gently but firmly, "By serving humanity, you serve me!"

Swami Sadasivananda

ॐ नमो नारायणाय

One day, after making a boat trip to Nassau, I returned to the *ashram* and, I thought, securely tied the boat to the dock. The next thing I knew, someone was asking if I was on boat duty and when I replied that I was, they instructed, "Swamiji wants to see you." They might as well have said: "The firing squad is ready." But strangely, when I got to the dock and saw Swamiji, he had already summoned two senior staff and was loudly telling them how he had found the boat tied only at one end. He did not even look at me as he suddenly found several other things wrong with moorings and security at the dock. He shouted for the two senior staff to get into the water and rectify the situation. They complied immediately. I felt embarrassed that I seemingly had caused the whole ruckus but was getting none of the heat.

That night at meditation, Swamiji recounted the incident and told how he examined himself afterwards. With astonishment in his voice and in his look he told how his devotees immediately, without question, obeyed his command to get into the waters of Nassau harbor and secure moorings. "What devotion!" he exclaimed. He said that not even in India one could find such devotion. Swamiji told the gathering that he had no control over these disciples. If they wished, they could easily say, "Bye-bye Swamiji" and leave him. But yet they stayed.

Swami Swyamananda

Often the task itself wasn't important. Swamiji would merely use the task to train you to think in a certain way, to prepare you for greater responsibilities. He always insisted that when you do something you do it to the absolute best of your abilities. He would accept no excuses for something done poorly or improperly.

Swamiji's dynamism knew no bounds. He literally wanted things done now. There was no question of waiting even for tomorrow despite the hour of the day or night. An interesting incident took place at a kibbutz in 1980 at the beginning of the first teachers' training course in Israel.

The director of Munich Centre had been invited to be with us at this inaugural course for 10 days. However, as it almost always seemed to happen with Swamiji, the plans changed. On a Friday evening, after the onset of the

Jewish Sabbath, Swamiji instructed me to put her on a flight to India right away. I explained to him that on the Sabbath all businesses were closed and the likelihood of a plane flying to India the next day was negligible. I also knew that India and Israel weren't on very good terms, so there were not many flights. But of course he insisted that I try.

Not only were businesses closed until Sunday morning but the only phone available was a lone pay phone requiring special tokens, only a few of which I had. The kibbutz was in the Negev miles away from the Tel Aviv centre. I could not say no to Swamiji so I did my best by calling our travel agent at home (fortunately she was one of our close yoga students and understood the urgency). But there were no flights at all that day, and only one per week. What about indirect flights through Turkey for example? No way at all. So I had to go back to Swamiji with this news. Only after proper research into the matter was he finally satisfied.

Swami Padmapadananda

ॐ नमो नारायणाय

In the Autumn of 1991, Swamiji went to India. I had just started to attend him during the nights and I also went on the trip. At that time Swamiji was still very strong, even though he was often not well. He was spending all his energy in teaching us mental discipline and attention in action.

On this trip I was given the responsibility of holding one portion of the money that we were taking for the whole trip. I could put some of the money into the money belt which I wore around my waist, the rest I kept in a small backpack that I took with me everywhere. Swamiji had warned several times, "If you lose your bag I will send you back to Canada." I would say, quite sure of myself, "No Swamiji I won't lose my bag."

So, for the whole trip it became a full sadhana to always watch my bag. It was not always an easy task. Swamiji was moving at lightening speed. The times when we were departing from one place or reaching another required particular attention. Swamiji had to be transferred from his wheelchair into the back of the car. Since the stroke Swamiji could only use the right side of his body. So, needless to say, this operation required one's full attention to avoid any injury to Swamiji and to make the transfer as comfortable for him as possible. As I had to hold Swamiji very closely for the transfer, I had to take my pack off my back. Often as I was holding Swamiji firmly around his back, watching his left hand so that it would not be banged, watching his head, and helping him to turn and sit, Swamiji would suddenly say to me, "Where is your bag? Watch your bag." I would answer "Yes Swamiji it is there with this person."

One day in Gangotri, Swamiji was sitting on his favorite spot just outside the door of the cave, contemplating the river. I was off duty and having dinner on the cement platform which is located a few yards below the cave. Suddenly I heard Swamiji call my name. I sprang to my feet and ran up towards him and said, "Yes Swamiji." He looked at me and said, "Atmaram, where is your bag?" I was startled. My bag had been right next to me as I was eating, but when Swamiji had called me I had run up and left it there. I realized that Swamiji was showing me that at any time my mind could get distracted.

Swami Atmaramananda

ॐ नमो नारायणाय

One of my first personal encounters with Swami Vishnu-devananda was in April, 1977, before the teacher training I was to take with him at the Camp. Swamiji was focusing his immense energies on his book *Meditation and Mantras*. In it, he translated his explosive lectures and vast knowledge into spoken word. He knew exactly what he wanted to say but not exactly how to say it. He already had two of his staff working night and day with him. When I volunteered that I had studied writing at the university, he immediately asked me to join the team. In his care for details, Swamiji would test us to see if we completely understood what he was saying. He also took the opportunity to teach us to think properly and to test us as an audience.

For Swamiji, the importance was one's potential, not limitations. A little discipline in any field, became the foundation for a vocation.

Srinivasan
Val Morin, PQ, Canada

Karma Yoga wasn't just for people who worked in the ashrams and teaching centers, but for all Swamiji's students, everywhere. It didn't matter what you did, the concepts of selfless service always applied.

I had many difficult moments caring for my late mother and father. Swamiji helped me endure these times and grow spiritually by what he wrote in my book on December 17, 1961:
"To Sri Annette,
Serve, Love, Give, Purify, Meditate, Realize. God is Truth. God is Love. Remember God at all times. There is no greater joy than serving the poor, sick and old. May Lord bless you."

Annette Celine Mizne
New York, NY

A True Saint

Swamiji never pretended to anything other than what he was, a man struggling to attain God-realization, trying to follow what Sivananda taught him, and constantly praying for God's help on the way. He never put on airs, and until very late in his life, discouraged anyone from worshipping him, insisting in all humility that anything he achieved was only through the grace of God. He wanted people to understand that anything they accomplished would likewise be through their own self-effort, that he could only guide them along the road, not take them there.

I'm not using any magic pills to bring you all here. I've only taught hard discipline, self-discipline; it's the only way I know. I've practiced all my life. I have no magic formula, no secrets. I've got no secret magic *mantras* in my hand. What I've learned is hard, selfless sacrifice. Even when I was four years old I had to walk four miles to school in the morning and four miles back; eight miles I had to walk. Often I could not carry my books or lunch because I had to cross the many rivers and streams swollen by the rain. I led a hard life. I never knew life was anything but discipline.

For two years I was in the military. Discipline again. I went to Master's *ashram* and there I also learned discipline. That's all I can give you; I can show you how to discipline yourself, how to be a master of your own destiny.

Your destiny is not in my hands nor in anyone else's. Your destiny is in your own hands. I can show you how to stand on your head, but I cannot do it for you. It's the same with your feet. You, yourself, must stand on your own feet. Only then can you help others. That's why you are here, to learn this discipline, to gain this knowledge. The greatest knowledge of yoga is that of discipline.

Discipline means controlling this wild horse, this wild mind. This is nothing secret. You don't have to go anywhere to learn that the enemy is within. The enemy you are fighting is not outside. Where is it? It's in your own mind. Mind alone is the cause of your bondage. Mind alone is the key to your liberation. How you use the mind determines the result.

I will guide you in whatever way I can. The only thing I want from you all is that you follow the teachings of Master Sivananda. He really cares. I lived with him and I watched his suffering. He didn't expect anything from anyone. All he did was give, give, give. "Serve, Love,

Give" was his motto. Follow this unselfish principle. Serve, love, give, purify, meditate. I can interpret his teachings a little bit, with my own weaknesses. I can show you some methods of controlling the mind through your own hard work. I can assure you that if you follow these teachings for controlling your own mind, then you'll reach a more peaceful state, which I can't describe.

When I come to you, I pray to the Master and I change my vibrations: "Don't make me egoistic; don't make me think that I know more than these people; just let me speak as an instrument, as your instrument; remove this ego, I am." That's all. So I say this prayer before I come. I offer flowers to the altar; I offer to Lord Siva, to *guru,* my teacher, to Lord Krishna, to Devi, and of course to disciples and to you all and I come to you and I also prostrate before you mentally. I do not think that you are just students.

So there is a pulling of the senses and the mind, the emotions to the center. I AM, the big I Am, not the small ego. Small ego is identified with the muscular body: "Oh, I am 155 pounds, the great Swami Vishnu." But the Self, Atman, the Center force is infinite. So when I remove the small ego, you can identify with the big ego. That's called God. That's all the whole of yoga is.

My purpose is not external show; anyone can put on an external appearance . It's very simple; it's illusion. As soon as I come here, all of my disciples will bow down before me and go "ooh ahh!" Each time when they come, suddenly, "ahhh!" I can make this show but still my mind will not be any better; it would be worse. Gurudev Sivananda, he never did that external show at all. He tried to remove the show business, religious hypocrisy. Others will come with the peacock feather, go and hit everybody; they make a line, and each of the disciples will come and be hit with the peacock feather. What kind of hypocrisy it is? As if he has got the power to hit everyone, give knowledge by hitting with a peacock feather. Do you understand these people's motives?

I don't come with ego. Even saying that is ego. If you say, "I don't come with ego," even that is ego. But still I have to use the word, you know, I just use the word because I do have ego. If I don't have ego, I wouldn't be able to talk to you. But I offer that ego also to God. Offer everything to God. That's called devotion. Without that devotion, you cannot move one step in the spiritual path, you cannot move at all; it's God's Grace.

ॐ नमो नारायणाय

Many saints seem saintly because they hide their human failings. Swamiji paraded his humanity and his faults.

He hid his saintliness, and thus showed us what ordinary human beings can accomplish.

Neela Devi
Washington, D.C.

It was this very ordinariness that attracted many students to Swamiji. He didn't try to make you feel that he was somehow different, or special. He neither demanded nor expected worship, in fact he actively discouraged it. You could, in some senses, just 'hang out' with Swamiji, be with him in normal, day to day situations, or what on the surface at least seemed to be normal life. Except there was always something special about these times, they had an "otherness" that made them somehow extra-ordinary.

Swamiji came to Ottawa for the day almost three weeks ago now, on April 8, 1985. He had an appointment at the Sports Medicine Clinic, to have his knee checked out. (A minor accident in the jeep, when he was being driven down from Gangotri, had reactivated an old injury.)

I didn't record the events of this day earlier, as in a way they seemed so mundane. Nothing special happened. As the weeks have gone by though, I realize the events of that day have left very lasting impressions.

This was the first time I'd seen Swamiji since his winter at the cave in Gangotri. He seemed thinner, frailer and very sweet.

He arrived accompanied by Swamis Kartikeyananda and Sitaramananda. It was a rainy cold day and a funny image of Swamiji's feet on the hall mat remains vivid. They were clad in heavy white cotton socks, inside big red-brown loafers, a few sizes too large to accommodate his toes, still healing from frost-bite.

I chauffeured Swamiji and company in our car to the clinic, then to the Indian High Commission, then back to the clinic again that afternoon. Each time he got into the car, he touched Master's picture on the dash, then touched his fingers to his forehead and said some prayers. This happened six times. The last time, he interrupted himself to tell me, "Start the car!" I thought I was supposed to wait until he finished praying.

Shortly after he arrived, Swamiji requested a sandwich. While he was eating it, some of the pulp and seeds of the tomatoes dripped out of the bottom and down the front of his orange sweater. It was a good-size spot, but he was quite oblivious to it and remained unnoticing right up until we were leaving for the clinic, at which point Swami Kartikeyananda took a napkin and tried to wipe it off. Swamiji just smiled and said, "See, even the tomatoes are attracted to me. They want to be with me."

Madalasa
Ottawa, Ontario

ॐ नमो नारायणाय

In the early days at the Sivananda Ashram in Val Morin, Swami Vishnu-devanandaji used to be present at all the ashram activities: evening and morning *satsangs*, *asana* classes, silent walks, etc. He used to tell us, if we come to the *ashram* we should fully merge ourselves in *ashram* activities without dissipating the energies outside. He used to add especially, "Don't go down to the village, to the diner. It's not the best place in the world, and it's a little too far away from the *ashram*."

One Sunday, another ashramite and myself were not quite happy with the 10 o'clock *ashram* food—some porridge and bread. So we decided to sneak out and go to visit this famous diner. We very casually walked away from the main gate, and then rushed to the restaurant, quite happy to be free and already drooling thinking of the pleasant food at the diner.

We opened the door, entered, and aaarrgghh!

Swamiji was sitting there, suitably dressed in T-shirt and shorts amongst 2 or 3 secretaries, answering the mail. He was having french fries, sugar pie with ice-cream and drinking tea. As soon as he saw us he invited us to sit with him and immediately with great care and a little mischievous look in his eyes, he asked "Do you want some fries and ice-cream?" Naturally, if any of us had a preconceived idea or naive notion of what a *guru* should look like, it was totally shattered then.

His look said, "Just because I'm not wearing swami dress and am sitting here eating fries and ice-cream, does it mean I'm not a *guru* anymore?"

Look not at appearances. Look at the spirit and motivation behind them.

Swami Mahadevananda

ॐ नमो नारायणाय

One time we were in the Vienna center. Swamiji was sitting in the asana room which on this day was filled with sunlight, an exception in Vienna. We had gotten a nice armchair and a table for Swamiji, where he could sit in the morning and read his newspaper.

He called me. When I entered the room, he looked at me and said, "You look radiant today. You must be doing something right."

I felt very embarrassed and all I could think was, "What was it I did to make it right?"

Swami Durgananda

ॐ नमो नारायणाय

One day Swamiji canceled classes, and we all piled into cars and buses and vans and went on a long drive. Then we had to hike down a path that led to a swimming hole and waterfalls. As usual, he literally flew down the path and we all had to scramble (even the young staff) to keep up with him.

He made us all swim, and he swam, and we sat under the falls. They were about 25 feet high, and some of the more daring dove off the falls into the water. Then Swamiji gave us a lecture on how we needed to be there that day because our minds had had enough of his lectures, and the hot sun.

Cathleen Clark
San Francisco, California

ॐ नमो नारायणाय

One spring at the yoga retreat I was lying asleep on my mat on the beach platform under the huge pines. Suddenly, feeling a light and warmth on me, I woke up with a start. There was Swami Vishnu, on the platform, beaming his radiant smile at me. I nervously started to get up, like a child caught doing something wrong. He put his hands together in a greeting, bent forward and let me know it was OK. I felt totally blessed, and sank back on the mat.

Silvia Goldsmith
New York City, New York

ॐ नमो नारायणाय

Several years ago I taught Swami Vishnu how to fly an ultra light plane. This was before he flew over the Berlin Wall on one of his peace missions. Swamiji was a great student. He listened carefully to everything I said with full concentration. He absorbed it all and learnt quickly, putting aside all his previous knowledge of flying bigger aircraft.

One day we couldn't fly because the winds were too high, so we sat around the airfield just talking and waiting. It was one of the best days of my life and one I'll always remember.

Ted Young
Ellenville, New York

Swamiji would often react very differently from those around him to situations that other people thought normal. He would experience things, particularly strongly emotional or violent things, much more intensely than everyone else around him. He often told the following story about Mohammed Ali.

I went to Miami for some work and heard that Mohammed Ali

was in training there. I wanted to see what kind of training boxers do. He was strong. His sparring partner took many punches, very strong punches. Ali kept giving them one after another. Occasionally he would lean against the rope. Why? He was resting. Because his breathing was very shallow, he wasn't able to get sufficient oxygen and a few of his powerful punches took tremendous energy.

After the fighting, I gave him an autographed copy of my book and said to him, "You know, your breathing is very shallow. You won't be able to fight long if you don't change your breathing pattern." I advised him in a friendly way, teaching him how to breathe and telling him, "Increase your breathing capacity if you want to survive."

Some time later I was in California. At that time there was a fight scheduled between Mohammed Ali and Joe Frazier. There was a huge indoor screen where one could watch the fight so some students said, "Swamiji, would you like to see Ali fight?" I answered that I wanted to see how he was breathing.

So on the big screen I watched Ali and Joe Frazier hit each other. Joe Frazier's blood was pouring out and Mohammed Ali's face became puffy. So many punches, so many times! Each time they hit each other I felt as if I was hit; I was the victim of that punch.

This hitting, hitting, hitting each other went on for an hour. Finally the fight was over. Ali won. The hall was lit. Everyone walked out. But I just sat in my seat; I could not move. I could not move at all. My stomach was churning with acid; I never in my life felt acid like that burning in my stomach. My legs were aching. My body was paralyzed. I sat there like a zombie. Everyone was gone except the two or three students who had come with me. They sat waiting for me to come out; they thought I was meditating. But I wasn't meditating; I was paralyzed. I literally could not get up and walk. At that time my body was in a very strong, healthy state, but for fifteen or twenty minutes I could not move. Afterwards, I had to drink two or three glasses of milk to dilute the acid in my stomach. It took at least three hours before I could relax or sleep.

Swamiji lived the idea of being one with all living beings. He was open to all and suffered when those around him felt any pain or sorrow.

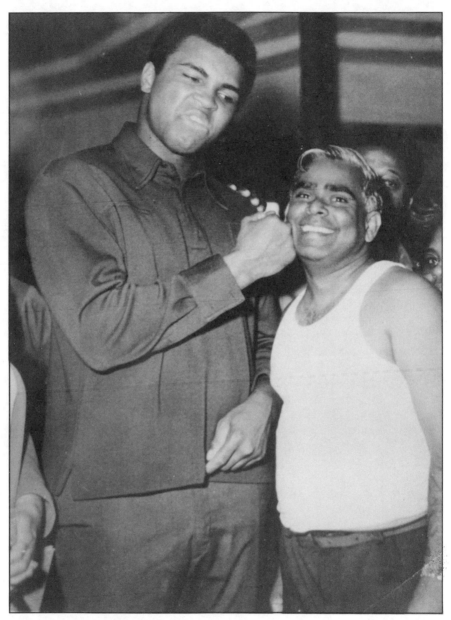

Swamiji with Muhammad Ali.

Relationships

Even though Swamiji never married, and was for most of his life a celibate sanyasin, he had a unique understanding of how people should relate to each other in a committed relationship. He would talk openly and freely about love and sex, and help people come to a clearer understanding of these topics in relation to their spiritual practice.

You should not experience guilt about sexual feelings. The entire universe is dependent upon sexual feeling. Otherwise there would be no world left. To go against sexual feelings is just like trying to climb up Niagara Falls. It is the great energy moving down from time immemorial. If it is forced shut, then it becomes stronger and rushes down. And to swim up the falls? There are only a few who can do that!. That's not completely possible on effort alone. We need God's grace.

Don't try to suppress the sexual feeling. It is not possible. But we can sublimate it. Just as water, when it is flowing, flows from higher to lower, but, when it is heated, goes upward, so sublimation is making the sexual energy like vapor. This vapor is called *ojas*. It goes upwards to the higher centers instead of going to the lower centers, the sexual center. Ordinarily, when sexual feelings come, our own effort is not sufficient to stop them. When you do *asanas*, when you do *pranayama*, when you do japa regularly and with the right diet, without onions and garlic and certain roots which over stimulate the nerves, then sublimation will take place little by little. That's when the energy starts moving to the upper *chakras* (psychic energy centers) and reaches the brain. This same sexual energy will now form a creative force, a positive spiritual force. That's why you see halos around the heads of sages and saints; it is the *ojas shakti* emanation. If a person has even partial control of the sexual energy, his face is different. He will never get wrinkles. The skin gets very dry and wrinkled when too much of the energy is wasted and made gross in the sexual act.

Both male and female have that psychic energy which comes down from the brain and then becomes gross. Once you learn to divert this energy and channel it in the opposite direction, it is no longer a sexual thing. Do you recall the story of Krishna and his

16,008 wives? All of them learned to control and to sublimate the energy. They each experienced union with Lord Krishna, but it was not a physical union; it occurred in a higher state.

The *gopis* were beautiful milkmaids so in love with Lord Krishna that they couldn't keep their eyes away from him even one minute. The *gopis* were tested to see whether they were able to sublimate this energy. They went to the Yamuna River one cold morning and prayed, "Let Lord Krishna be my husband." Then they went to bathe in the river. Lord Krishna came and took all their clothes which they had left on the river bank and put them on the top of a tree. Then he started to play the flute. The girls all looked up to see him and discovered that he had tied each one's clothes neatly, each on a different branch. They were cold and could not stay naked in the river for too long. They had to come out, so they begged him, "Oh Krishna, give us our clothes. Why are you naughty? Why are you doing this thing?" He said, "If you want them, you can come and get them. I'll stay here and I'll give you your clothes. Just come out of the water." But they resisted. "O.K., then you can stay out in the cold." At last when they could not stand it any longer, they began to come out, with hands covering their private parts. But Krishna said, "No, no. You have to let both hands drop." When they threatened to tell his mother and his father, he said, "O.K., tell them if you want. That will not bring your clothes to you." At last they surrendered to Lord Krishna, raised their hands and came out.

Lord Krishna was not really trying to do any kind of mischief. The *gopis* wanted the Lord to be their husband but Krishna is not a human being. If the Lord is to be their husband, they must not think that they are women and he is a man. They must forget their body consciousness. They must transcend the body consciousness. Male and female is only imagination. Today you can be Mister but tomorrow, after an operation, you can be Miss. It happens every day. But the Atman is the Immortal Self with which you are going to unite.

The *saguna* form of *Brahman* (God with form or attributes) is Krishna or Rama, and if you want to unite with him, you can't think, "I am a male", or, "I am a female. I am coming to you and you must be my husband." So Krishna, when he heard the Gopis' prayer, said, "You are not ready." Every day the Gopis went and meditated in the cold morning. Krishna knew that they were transcending the body, but still they had a little ego; their female egos continued to exist. So long as they did not remove that female ego and so long as they continued to think that he was just a male to be their husband, they were not ready to be united.

That's the whole significance behind this story. When they lost their body consciousness, the Lord said, "On the full moon you will hear my flute. You will come to Vrindavan, and you will have the cosmic dance with me."

So, sexual feeling is difficult to conquer unless and until you convert that emotion into devotion to God. Nuns, for example, stay single but they believe they are married to Jesus. It is not a sexual marriage; it is a divine marriage. They connect themselves to Jesus so that they will somehow be able to sublimate that energy.

The sexual feeling comes to all. Guilt shows that you know that something you are doing is not being done in the right way. When you have a guilty feeling, repeat God's name and surrender again, "Thy will be done oh Lord. I did my level best and now it's up to you. I can't help myself. I can't do anything."

It is the same with swami's lives, you know. This energy is very difficult to conquer. Every sage and saint and yogi in the Himalayas had problems. It is not only you who has this problem. Because they go into the Himalayan caves it means that this problem will go away? It rather multiplies.

So don't worry about this feeling; sublimate it. Repeat your Mantra each time, and if this feeling comes even then, offer it as an offering to God. That's the only way we can help you, no other way. If anyone says that he has conquered sex, he is not true to himself nor true to the world. It takes till the last breath. You never know when maya will attack you. Even if you are a hundred-year-old man, it still can overcome your thinking.

Swamiji never pretended that he was better than others, or above certain problems, just because he was a *sanyasin* and had taken a vow of chastity. He was very accepting of his many householder disciples and never put them down because they weren't capable of or interested in following the path he'd chosen.

> The first time I ever went to Swamiji with a personal problem was when I was struggling with the whole idea of celibacy. I had somehow gotten to the point in my mind where I thought that if I was going to make any spiritual progress I had to take Bramacharya (a vow of celibacy), but I was in no way prepared to do so. I told Swamiji that I felt guilty for not following the "right" path. Swamiji just smiled at me gently and said, "Even the great rishis had wives and had sex with them." He went on to explain that as a householder celibacy was not expected of me. What was more important was my attitude towards my wife. I should see her not as just a woman, but as an incarnation of the Goddess. I should always think of her and treat her worshipfully. If I could do that then being a householder would make no difference to my spiritual progress.
>
> Gopala Krishna
> Ottawa, Ontario, Canada

ॐ नमो नारायणाय

When I was trying to spiritualize my sexual relations, Swamiji counseled me, "Sex and yoga are two different things. If you want to have sex, enjoy it, but don't try and make it yoga." So I don't, and it works great.

Sarabess Forster
Silver Springs, Maryland

Swamiji actively supported his householder disciples, encouraging them and reminding them of their duties to each other. He was always genuinely interested in the welfare of all members of the family.

My husband Jim and I were married by Swamiji. He personally conducted a beautiful fire ceremony. He gave a talk extolling the benefits and beauties of the householder life. Our relatives, who had started off a little uncomfortable at the strangeness of the ceremony, were touched and moved and warmed by Swamiji's love and enthusiasm.

Once when I was driving Swamiji from the New York center to the yoga ranch, a two hour drive, I asked him for help with a problem. I went into a long discourse about how Jim wasn't as committed to being staff at the ranch as I was and how this caused tensions, etc., etc. Though I had been shy in the beginning, once I began I went on for a long time. When I finally stopped Swamiji turned to me and said, "Sorry, what did you say?" I was a bit stunned but then realized that I was already feeling better and that now I could more concisely explain the situation. Afterwards Swamiji told me not to worry and to pray to God.

When we pulled into the ranch driveway Jim was there and Swamiji immediately began to encourage and love him. The whole time Swamiji was at the Ranch he gave Jim extra attention. At one *satsang* he called Jim to the front and had him read "The Rules for Being Human" from a recent issue of *Yoga Life*. After each rule Swamiji would turn and speak directly to Jim as he explained about living life fully and beautifully without forgetting God. He didn't scold or admonish Jim. He gave only pure love and concern. After *satsang* he told Jim to sleep with that *Yoga Life* under his pillow. Jim did. Later we moved it under the bed. It is still there after seven years.

Over the years Swamiji never failed to ask me "How is Jim?" Once when I visited the Val Morin *ashram* I went to greet Swamiji who was sitting alone at a picnic bench. He was in *mouna*, so he wouldn't talk, but he began to trace some letters to make a word on the bench. After some hesitation I realized he was spelling h-u-s-b-a-n-d. Another reminder of duty came when Swamiji was departing from the ranch after a brief visit. Swamiji was lying in the back seat of the car and I bent in to touch his feet and say good-bye. He said something to me, but this was after he had his strokes and his speech was difficult to understand. I guessed, "Keep up with your sadhana?" Swamiji shook his head no. "Work hard at the *ashram*?" No, that wasn't it either. I guessed and guessed until Swami Kartikeyananda got into the car and translated, "Where is Jim? Has he gone to work?" Again Swamiji was reminding me to think of my husband! That was the constant message.

The last time Swamiji came to the ranch he was quite weak but as usual beautiful, accessible and concerned for all. Jim and I had been thinking about having children but had many doubts about it. I wanted very much to talk to Swamiji about it, and I knew we would follow whatever he said. I told Swamiji about our confusion about having children. Swamiji immediately replied, "Why not?" I replied that our Sadhana would change and that I wouldn't be able to help at the *ashram* as much. The main focus would be on the children. I wasn't sure because it would be such a big change. Swamiji responded by saying, "Even Lord Rama had children. The highest good is to train children properly, and to bring them up in an *ashram* is a great blessing."

Lisa
Woodbourne, NY

ॐ नमो नारायणाय

On September 22nd, 1992, my wife and I visited Swamiji in his house in Val Morin. Though he could not speak clearly because of his paralysis, he inquired about my children with his sign language and his eyes. He prayed for us, as if he could visualize something was going to happen to us soon. Early on the morning of September 26th my son Sandeep left his body in a car accident.

Shambu Das
Toronto, ON, Canada

The Physical Presence

There is something special about being in the presence of someone who has made progress along the spiritual path. Just being in the same physical space with them, even if they don't say or do anything, often has a profound affect on people. Why do great yogis and sages affect people so strongly? Swamiji explained it this way.

Flexibility of the body, especially the spinal cord, and flexibility of the mind are interrelated. Flexibility of the mind means adaptability. Its opposite, rigidity of mind, is called ego. As ego puts stress upon the nervous system, it creates a rigid body. So yoga says that flexibility of the spine and flexibility of the mind are interrelated. If you keep the spinal column flexible, you'll have a flexible mind, and you will find that the flexible mind can do more work than the inflexible mind.

Have you ever seen a tree standing on the shore? Such trees are very strong, still standing after 70, 80 or 90 years. When a sudden flood comes, they are completely uprooted and washed away because they are very rigid. When the flood waters subside, the tall grasses are still there. The powerful flood waters could not wash them away. Why? Because they just bent with the flow of the waters instead of resisting. The water could not do anything. However, the more powerful but rigid tree was uprooted.

Grasses blow before the gale and again raise their heads to the midday sun. The proud giants of the forest remain stiff, not budging an inch, only to be rudely uprooted. The humble servant prostrates to all and goes on serving until retired by old age, while his unbending master is envied, only to be thrown out as Prime Minister or Senator, or even disgraced and thrown in prison. But the ordinary servant goes on.

For a spiritual aspirant especially, flexibility is necessary. Once the prana starts growing, any resistance will prevent its free movement. So every morning you should practice your *asanas* (yoga postures), *pranayama* (breathing exercises), and *mantra japa* (repetition of God's name). Flexibility of the spinal column will allow the energy to flow properly, so that instead of going downward, it will go upward. It is just like water, which, in a gross

state, flows downwards, but when in subtle form (as in steam) it
rises. In the same way, a flexible spinal cord will allow your
energy to flow upward, past the lower centers and up to the higher
centers. That is what is meant by the "ascent of *kundalini shakti*."

The *shakti*, or energy, which is stored in your lower chakras, is
called *kundalini*. It is like the spring in a watch, tightly coiled from
being wound, so that when released, it makes the watch hands
move. The energy is condensed, it is potential. *Kundalini* is coiled
up and lying in a dormant state for most of us. Through the
performance of *asanas*, and *pranayama* it unwinds, releases, and
raises up to the higher centers. As it is stimulated, each center (or
chakra) releases a specific wavelength of energy stored in it like a
battery. As you rise, the voltage increases. The lower *chakras* may
have say only six volts, but as go up, you encounter ten, fifty, a
hundred, a thousand volts. So, for spiritual evolution, it is
important to raise the energy to the higher centers. Now you can
see the interrelationship between your physical body and
physical-mental flexibility. We perform all the physical exercises
to get mental flexibility and to get the energy moving properly,
removing blockages in the centers.

Yoga is primarily a spiritual discipline that has an outward physical component.
The practice of yoga is like a flower. What we can see—the physical process and its
effects on the body—is very beautiful. But that beauty is supported by the flowers
strong invisible roots. Cut off the roots and the flower quickly withers and dies.
Similarly, the physical practice of yoga separated from its spiritual roots quickly
becomes distorted and meaningless.

What is the benefit of focusing not only on the physical process but on the
spiritual underpinnings of *yoga sadhana*? First we must remember that the word
yoga itself means union, the coming together of the higher self, the soul, and God.
This state of oneness with God has many different names in different traditions;
nirvana, samadhi, Christ-consciousness. All traditions agree however that
whatever the name, achieving this state is the goal of life, the primary duty of all
human beings.

What happens when we reach this state of union with God? Swamiji used to say
that answering this question is like trying to describe to someone who has never
tasted honey what honey tastes like. We can say it is sweet, like sugar. It is sort of
like corn syrup in texture, but without the corn taste, and so on. No matter how
hard we try we cannot explain what honey tastes like to someone who has never
tasted it. Put one drop of honey on that persons tongue however, and the need for
explanation vanishes. They simply 'know' now, without any need for explanation.
So it is with *samadhi*. We can verbally dance around the idea, we can use analogy,
but it can never really be explained. It can only be experienced.

Why is achieving this spiritual goal so important? It sounds so wishy-washy and
vague. If we can't understand it, if it so irrational, what possible good could come
from being in this state? Since we can't understand it intellectually, perhaps we

should look at what outward effect achieving God-realization has on someone. What did Swamiji have to say about the external results of this internal process?

> When the energy is moving properly, you are bound to get healthy, strong, and peaceful, radiating strength and vitality to others; to your family, to your loved ones, to your friends. Then, wherever you go, whomever you meet, they will all draw energy from you; you'll be the center of attraction and everyone will want to touch you, to shake hands with you, to be with you. Even your mere presence will bring them energy and strength.

If you have ever been in the presence of someone who is God-realized, or is even well established on the path, you will immediately understand what Swamiji means here. There is an incredible feeling of peace and well-being that you experience when you are with someone who radiates this spiritual energy. This feeling of being one with God is something that everyone is looking for and needs. It is the only true source of happiness in this world.

Swamiji certainly radiated strength and vitality to others. Just being in the same space with him often had a strong effect on people. Even when he was silent by choice (earlier on when he went through periods of *mouna*), or latter after his stroke (when he spoke little or not at all), he touched people in some undefined but profound way. He taught not by what he said, but by who he was.

From a student's journal of the Sivananda Centenary Tour, India, 1987:

> Today has been a wonderful day. We were able to spend most of the day at the Divine Life Society *ashram*. We took the bus there first thing this morning. Swamiji took us to the library, where we had a short *satsang*. Even in the library, which is not one of the most sacred buildings, the peace is so deep. Once you close your eyes, you just don't want to open them. When you open them, the physical manifestations of Master Sivananda surround you: large photographs, mottoes hung on the walls — "Hate none. Hurt none." "The same Lord dwells in all." So, eyes opened or closed, Master is there. The whole space is full of Master. Just sitting under the tree where Master had often sat, watching the life of the *ashram* going on all around, we had a real sense of meeting up with part of a personal history. For the first time since we arrived in India, I felt completely at home. On the streets, in the cities, we saw many things that were incomprehensible to me. Here, everything made sense. Of course, that's due to all the time we've spent at the Val Morin *ashram* with Swamiji. He has prepared us well, and explained so much about Master's ways.
>
> About 3:00, *kirtan* (mantra chanting) started in the *mahasamadhi* shrine. Went in and chanted for an hour. Could feel both the devotion of all the people going out with the chant, and Master's love flowing back from the shrine, just like overlapping waves, electrifying.
>
> After dark everyone went down to the Ganges for the Ganga *arati* (worship of the Ganges) Swamiji had arranged. Swamiji had invited everyone at the *ashram* to attend, and an announcement of this had been made in the

Swamiji sitting quietly with his pet goat, Kiddie.

conference hall, so there was a huge rush and crush, maybe a thousand people, all going down some very narrow alleys and crooked flights of stairs, to get to the river. Everyone was chanting *Om Namo Narayanaya*. It was a beautiful sight, watching the mantra boats floating down the river, starting one by one as isolated points of fire, then farther away looking like one continuous ribbon of light.

There was no time to stand and absorb this though, to enter into the feeling of the arati. The minute your succeeded in launching your boat, it was necessary to turn and start elbowing your way back up the stairs, or risk winding up right in the Ganges along with the boats, as the next wave of people continued to press down, boats in hand.

This experience really made me appreciate the intimacy of the small *satsang* we are often able to have with Swamiji at Val Morin, once the summer season is over. So many seekers are at the *ashram* here now. How many people can have that kind of personal experience of a teacher, extending over years? It is really a gift.

September 12, 13, 14, 1987, Sivananda Guha, Gangotri

It has been just like one continuous day since we got here, a magical place and time cut off from everything else. Most of the people on the trip are staying in the little village of Gangotri itself, about a fifteen minute walk from the cave. A small group, mostly staff from the various centers, are staying in the cave compound, sleeping either in tents or in one of two small caves.

I have never lived in a cave before. It's amazing how your eyes can adjust. When you first walk in, it's pitch black, but after closing your eyes and opening them again, you can see many details clearly. Sleeping here gives a tremendous feeling of strength and security. You are really tucked away, and the walls couldn't be more solid.

Swamiji has urged lots of pranayama and individual meditation during our stay here, and really, there can't be many places more conducive to both. The altitude, the fresh air and forests, and the icy cold Ganges make a natural environment full of *prana*. Added to this is the *ashram* environment, not just Swamiji's cave but all the little caves, huts and shrines along the Ganges banks.

I can understand so much better now the fusion of spiritual and practical activities which is such an integral part of the Hindu mentality. Here, there is really no difference. You wake up in the morning and go down to the Ganges to wash. Before washing, offer a prayer to the river. The bath is both worship and hygiene. Wash out a few pieces of clothing and spread them on the rocks to dry in the sun. You have to wait for them to dry, so there's no better time to choose a flat rock close by and do some pranayama. Meditation comes by itself, with the roar of the Ganges blocking out any other sound.

Since most of the others have gone off on an overnight hike, it is like *satsang* all day long around here. Swamiji has been outside often, sharing little conversations and taking his mid-day meal outdoors with us.

At the conclusion of the meal, during which everyone was in very high spirits, Swamiji had a *chapatti* left on his plate. He asked, "Who wants this?" Before anyone answered, he turned to me and said, "Offer it to everyone." I took the *chapatti* around on the tray to each of the people that were present. The different reactions were interesting. Some people saw a cold, greasy *chapatti* and said, "I'm full, thanks." Other people saw *prasad* (blessed food), and immediately tore off a piece and ate it.

Following this, Swamiji simply turned on his side and lay down to snooze in the sun on a large stone slab. It's a hard thing for me to understand, but Swamiji doesn't have to do anything or say anything. Just to sit quietly within a certain radius of that body is to feel the sweetest peace.

September 22, 1987 Hotel Indraprastha, Palghat

After twelve hours on the bus, we arrived at our hotel in Palghat just after dark, to find the power out, due to evening power cuts. In the windowless hallways, it was impossible to see the numbers on the doors, so we sort of felt our way down the hall, reading the numbers on the second floor doors like Braille, until we arrived at 206.

We changed quickly and went right out again to meet Swamiji at the evening function at the Sivananda Ashram, Palghat. Swamiji was already talking when we arrived and some of our group were giving a very impromptu asana demonstration. The hall was jammed with about 600 people sitting on the floor and standing around the edges. More people were milling around outside. The resident swami gave a speech in Malayalam which everyone who understood seemed to find very funny—something about the flying swami being grounded.

Swamiji spoke briefly about Master's concept of integral yoga and then concluded with a very spirited *kirtan*. After *arati*, the crowd pressed up to touch his feet as he stood on the edge of the stage. There was a potential for things to get very emotional, but Swamiji just kept smoothing things out by steadily chanting *Om Namo Narayanaya* quietly, with his eyes closed, as wave after wave of people came up.

> Madalasa
> Ottawa, Ontario, Canada

ॐ नमो नारायणाय

Another Journal from the same period.

Outside the Ganges rushes past, crashing over boulders in the gorge below this hostel. Here we have the bare necessities, and the best food yet, miraculously produced by the Hotel Interlok staff on what looks like a portable stove, and with water brought up from the river. This morning, our first here, many of us were sick. Some were just too old to take the altitude. Some just disliked our rugged accommodations. Seven returned to Rishikesh. I did what I could to help the sick, and then after breakfast I headed up the river to Swamiji's kutir. I was hoping he'd let me do sadhana by his cave.

On my way I passed the 20 or so people who'd spent the night either in the caves or in tents outside. They told me to turn back, that we were going to take a group hike to some waterfalls, but I ignored them. Finally, I reached Swamiji's cave. I found him sitting on the bench outside the *guha*. He bowed to me with a beautiful, loving smile. "Go eat breakfast," he said.

It seems he is always telling me to eat! But I told him I'd eaten already. "Swamiji, I want to bathe."

"Yes, yes—meditate, relax, enjoy the sun." And so with his blessing I bathed in the icy river, and spent an hour and a half sitting on a rock out in the Ganges doing *pranayama* and meditating.

As I meditated, I felt that the Ganges was flowing right through me. Afterwards, I sat in the shelter of a huge boulder and ate an apple. I felt like a little child, safely nestled against Mother's flanks, without a worry in the world. I was conscious only of the divine love I felt pouring into me from the mountains, from the sky, from Ganga, and from Swamiji. He made a special allowance for me, beloved *Guru*, and let me stay near his guha when all but his immediate staff were absent.

> Saraswati
> New York, NY

ॐ नमो नारायणाय

For me the most interesting characteristic of Swamiji was that he never ceased to be the best example of how things should be done. By the very way he was acting, yoga became a living principle.

One time I remember clearly is New Year's Day, 1993 at the *ashram* in Val Morin. The morning was very clear, with radiant sunshine, but it was icy cold. At breakfast Swamiji announced that he wanted to go for a pilgrimage, a walk around the *ashram* grounds, to offer flowers, incense and prayers at the different temples. Everybody was invited to join. This was Swamiji's way of asking for God's blessing for the New Year. Like always in the last years, Swamiji's health was very poor, and of course he was sitting in a wheelchair.

I must confess that I would never have thought of going for a walk in the snow on this icy cold morning to ask for the grace of God but luckily, there was Swamiji, sitting in his wheelchair, unable to move his body. The thought came immediately, "If he can do it, if it's not to cold for him…"

Swamiji was dressed to go outside: a blanket to sit on, an extra blanket to sit on, double blanket to cover him, double hat on his head, mittens, double socks. He was asked several times if he really wanted to go. He insisted. So we went, and of course it was the best start to the New Year. I would have missed this wonderful opportunity without Swamiji being there.

In a way I felt ashamed. I was in good health, able to walk, and twenty years younger than Swamiji, but I would have felt it was too cold to go on the pilgrimage. One more time Swamiji had shown me that external conditions, physical conditions included, may not and cannot be an obstacle to performing one's duty, be it everyday work or the worship of

God. I cannot express how thankful I am that I have had the blessing of learning from Swamiji, mostly by just looking at him and the way he acted.

Swami Yajnavalkyananda

ॐ नमो नारायणाय

I was finishing up at the admissions hut at the Nassau *ashram* when Swami Vishnu appeared on one of the paths. He walked about, observing everything, greeting all, giving instructions. The staff introduced me, explaining to him that Kanti Devi had sent me from Uruguay.

He replied "Ah, Kanti Devi, Kanti Devi. . ." I did not speak English. I did not need to. His presence, his eyes, his gestures, his vibrations were enough.

The Teacher Training Course was under his direction; talks, meditations, passing on the teachings. An intense first week, where Swamiji joined us for walks, laughed, played, experienced everything. Saturday night at the talent show was like being with our Daddy, sharing good times.

The days passed. Swamiji was the center, the connection, the presence, although he wasn't always in our midst. Then came the time to leave. The memory of his last words are still in my heart. "The *ashram* is in your heart, close your eyes and you will be there whenever you want." I never needed to talk with Swamiji. To see him was enough to understand and comprehend what he was saying. Here and now I close my eyes and he is in my heart.

Vishnu
Montevideo, Uruguay

ॐ नमो नारायणाय

One weekend when arriving at the Yoga Ranch, my mind was very frazzled and mixed up, being tired from a long hectic week in the New York Center. I was pacing in the hallway in the main house, and Swami Kartikeyananda looked out of the dining room and pulled me in, where Swamiji was lying down. Immediately my mind became completely blank. It was as if Swamiji had taken an eraser and wiped out all the thoughts. I did not have to do a thing to be uplifted, but be there!

Swami Gajananamananda

ॐ नमो नारायणाय

Swamiji looked at me and saw all that is imperfect. There was no place to hide. But it was not with eyes of reproach that he looked at me. His eyes did not put me down or make me feel small or limited. His gaze was also not indulgent. It was without judgment, simply seeing what is.

Swamiji's eyes inspired me to do better. In them, I could see the difference between perfection and imperfection and the path to attain perfection.

Swami Sitaramananda

Devotion

Swamiji encouraged everyone to express their devotion to God by following whatever religious practices they felt comfortable with. He always said that yoga itself was not a religion but a way of life that could accommodate one's religious beliefs. He insisted that at their root all religions say essentially the same thing, that there is only one God, and that the apparent differences amongst religions were only in the form of worship. He also stressed that no one religion was better than any other, that no one religion was right for everyone, and that one needed to be careful not to get drawn into sectarian or exclusivist ways of thinking and acting.

Natural evolution can be enhanced, increased in a very short life span in this particular existence. We're all moving in the same direction and that direction is towards God, or, Godhead, whatever you want to call it.

It is raining today and the rain falls on a wide area, from the top to the bottom of the mountains and all in between, on trees, ponds and grass. These waters slowly, slowly collect and become small streams, and the small streams eventually will wind up in the bigger rivers. The rivers will slowly carry the same water to the rapids, through mountains and rocks, through difficult ways, breaking new paths around obstacles. The turbulent river winds up in the vast ocean. Its journey has stopped; no more turbulence. No more running all the time as it had since leaving the mountains, traveling thousands of miles through every type of terrain, in many different conditions, overcoming various obstacles. Through all this the restless river was constantly moving towards the source, from where it first came. That is the ocean. The ocean became water vapor and then formed clouds, and when it became cumulo-nimbus it drifted into different parts of the globe, and then came back again to the earth as rain.

The water was not happy to be either in the sky or on the mountain top: it was restless. It wanted to reach back to its source, the ocean. Only then, when that river reaches that source, does it become again majestic, universal. It has lost its name and form. This river that comes from Himalayas, called Ganges, when it arrives in the eastern part of India after journeying 3,000 miles, when it merges with the ocean, it looses its name as well as its form. It is no longer called the Ganges; it no longer has form. It becomes merged in the vast ocean; its name, its form, its qualities are lost. So also the Colorado River, the Mississippi River, the Nile, all rivers arrive at the ocean, and when they arrive—it doesn't matter where from—they all lose name and form. No one calls it the Colorado River now, or the Mississippi, or the Ganges. It is just one ocean. No one claims, "Oh, this is my holy Ganges. I love it! I worship my holy Ganges." Others worship some other river, they love it. But here no one can claim, "It is mine." It has become universal.

In yoga and vedanta that universal experience is called God-realization or, if you don't want to believe in God, Self-realization. With the ordinary human mind, the ordinary human intellect, we cannot grasp that infinite ocean: how big it is, how tall it is, how deep it is, how far away. With his ordinary senses, a man cannot see the end of the ocean, how wide and how deep it is, how many millions and millions of creatures live there, what turbulence takes place. None of this can we grasp through our senses by looking at the sea. So if it is so difficult to fathom the ordinary ocean with our senses, mind and intellect, how can we think of God?

God's infinite nature is far beyond our understanding. So-called religious leaders, especially fanatics, speak of God as if God is on their side; they don't understand God's infinite nature. God is not on the Russian side or the American side nor is He for Muslims, Israelis or Hindus. God is one infinite ocean of love, compassion, mercy, truth, joy, peace. We cannot measure how big he is, how compassionate that supreme being is. Nor can we measure this infinite creation which he made.

Even though many of you are educated, most of you still think God created only this planet earth, maybe the sun and Moon. And on this planet earth, he took quite a long time to create you people. He created Adam and Eve and they would not behave properly. They ate the apple and then they multiplied the population of this planet earth. Then came a few million Jews, a few million Christians, a few million Hindus, Arabs, Americans, Russians, etc. So now there are about five billion human beings on this planet earth. And then we divided that God into different sections: Hindu God, Christian God, Catholic god, Protestant God, Israeli God, Muslim God, Buddhist God. That is not God. We divided that Supreme Being and made him a finite object.

That God, that infinite being which we cannot realize through our intellects or through our minds, is divided up to suit our mental conditions. We push that Supreme Being into a small, tiny envelope. A Hindu thinks, "God is only to protect me, because I am a Hindu. I worship Lord Krishna, and so Krishna is only going to help me, a Hindu who worships Krishna; and maybe the Hare Krishna people too. They also worship Krishna." But Krishna won't help Christians, Muslims, Jews, Arabs, Russians, believers, non-believers, because they don't call his name as Krishna. So Muslims say, "Oh no! No, no! God's name is Allah, not Krishna. Your Krishna is nothing. Our Allah is the Supreme God. He will protect only Muslims or those who call him Allah and worship him the way the Muslims worship. Otherwise Allah is not going to help you. He is going to destroy you. So join my club." And Israelis and Jewish people, "Oh no, no, no! God is on our side. Unless and until you follow this particular path, God is not going to give you any salvation." Protestants say, "Oh no, no. No! That is not true! We've got one Supreme Father and Jesus came and only through him will you realize God. So join our club."

Each religious leader came and said "God is One, and he's on my side. Every religion—Christianity, Judaism, Mohamedism, Hinduism—it doesn't matter. They all say that there is only one God. But, when you worship that God, "Oh no! We're divided. That is not one God. The Hindu God is different from the Christian or the Jewish God." That is ignorance. That is not the purpose of yoga and vedanta.

Remember the river. The Ganges merges with the ocean, and that ocean contains water from thousands of rivers from around the globe. Not only do the waters of the holy Ganges enter that ocean, but also the waters of rivers which are not worshipped, which are used for fishing, which are polluted and unholy. When they come the ocean does not distinguish the holy Hindu water. The polluted river and the holy river become one. It's that way with God-realization.

Differentiation is a contradiction of yoga and vedanta. If you remove these ideas: "I am different from you, My religion is different from yours, My God is different from yours," then you have yoga and vedanta. Because people are unable to remove this differentiation, we are in our present state on this planet earth, in this particular time in history. Man has reached such a state that he is nearly dead. The rope is around his neck. He is standing on the very tips of his toes. The table is unsteady beneath him. Any moment, he'll be hanged. The human race is doomed unless some divine power comes to save us directly. And that divine power will come not come to save Hindus only, or Jews, or Christians, or Muslims, or any other group. That divine power, like the ocean, will contain all.

Swamiji always taught the universality of all religions, and the need for devotional practices. Even though he was a Hindu by birth, he didn't limit himself to any particular religious practice. Catholic Mass was often celebrated at Christmas and Easter. A Baptist choir regularly came and sang at the yoga retreat in Nassau. Rabbi Shlomo Karlbach would come and lead us in song and dance. At the Yoga Ranch in Woodbourne, Native American sweat lodges were often held.

People are emotional by nature, and have a need to express this side of themselves. Swamiji encouraged us to transmute our emotional nature, which we would express to other individuals, into *bhakti* (devotion), expressing love for God. At twice daily *satsangs* we chanted mantras, singing God's names. Religious holidays were celebrated with special pujas. The *ashrams* were all filled with shrines and temples.

Swamiji never hesitated to express his own devotion. He would often burst into tears when he heard the *Bhagavatam* chanted, or when students put on devotional plays depicting the lives of Krishna, Rama and other figures from the scriptures. Swamiji also regularly went on pilgrimages, especially in his later years, when his devotion to the Divine Mother grew stronger and stronger.

Himalayan Pilgrimage

"The purpose of pilgrimage is purification", said Swamiji, sitting at his favorite place on the left side of the little entrance to his cave "Sivananda Guha" facing the noisy and tumultuous Ganges and the gigantic rocky mountains. "I have all the facilities in the world, Nassau, New York, Canada etc., but nothing compares to this, exclaimed Swamiji. "I have to come all the way here to sit on the banks of Mother Ganges!"

Purification. Letting go our ideas, attachments, all these little worms and insects of our thoughts that are eating us alive, day and night. Letting go and finding Peace. Breathe in this wonderful, magic energy that invigorates and makes one feel and taste each and every moment as unique and eternal.

Unique and eternal this little village of Gangotri, Tibetan like with its old rock and wooden bundles of houses, its narrow village roads bordered by tiny sheds, bazaars and shops selling religious items, sweets, offerings, bottles for Ganges water. Unique and eternal this old temple of Mother Ganges where Swamiji first brought us, to prostrate to the Mother, receive prasad from the *pujari*, walk around the temple one to three times, and receive her blessings. Unique and eternal this walk on the bank of the river, among the polished rocks, on her (very holy, Swamiji said) gray sand, in the chilly Himalayan wind.

"One will have all sins washed away with one dip in Mother Ganges at Gangotri" (the last village on the road up the Ganges gorge), is the common belief. "How about one dip at Gomukh (the source of the Ganges, about 15 miles past Gangotri, and up another 5000 feet)?" Maybe all sins of this life and past lives, for the water is icy cold, just coming out from the glacier.

"You must have very good karma to be able to come here from that far, to have this dip in the Ganges", Swamiji said. So many people dream to do so and they can not come, even those who live in India. What else do you want? Being in the vibrations of saints and sages. Walking on their footsteps. Being in

Swamiji plays tablas.

their presence. One feels so tiny and insignificant visiting these holy places, these holy temples!

Visiting temples is seeing with our physical eyes the glories, colors and light of our inner temple. Ascending their hills and climbing their steps is like ascending, climbing the inner steps to the temple of our heart. Walking through dark labyrinths and solemn interior courts of the temples, preparing oneself to reach the core, and having *darshan* of the Lord! Be face to face with his glories!

Thus, guided by mysterious forces, without advance planning, Swamiji arrived unexpectedly to Kedarnath via GauriKund, where the Mandakini river is singing and where the cars stopped. It took us five hours by horse to reach the top. We had to climb 1800 meters up on 17 kilometers of trail. We rode on the horses and they walked slowly in queue following the young boys, their guides.

"What a karma to be a horse! Isn't it Swamiji?" asked C.P., our companion. "It is all God's *lila,*" whispered Swamiji. And he continues: "The one on top, the one under, the one in front are one. Who carries whom and who guides whom?"

After a few *chai* (hot tea) shops, we slowly approached the abode of Lord Shiva. The spectacle was very elevating. The mountain slopes were covered with a luxurious deep tropical vegetation, crossed by long streams and waterfalls. Finally we reached Kedarnath and walked to the temple.

What the eyes see in the core part of the temple is the triangular form of a black rock pointing from the ground. What the mind recognizes is the holy Sivalingam installed by Sri Adi *Guru* Sankaracharya. What the heart feels is acute devotion, the eyes want to swallow this beloved vision, ears filled with these unearthly chants and hymns. Swamiji was made to sit just next to the Sivalingam for puja. He sat cross legged and meditated while we performed a worship ceremony. His body trembled and tears and cries came out. His hands were folded in prayer and supplication gesture. What he saw, we never know, and he can never describe. All we know is this blissful and foreign expression of his face when he tried to describe it in these words: "It took me 60 years of my life to have this vision. It is indescribable the vision of Siva and Parvati in union, Cosmic Father and Cosmic Mother. It is like Mother and Father are waiting for me to come this moment to give me this vision."

Two days later, during the early morning puja at Badrinath, the holiest of the holy temples of India, the same thing happened to Swamiji. He did not talk much about it except telling the chief priest of the temple, the Rawal, a Kerala man, in office for 25 years, how beautiful Lord Badri Narayan was. He was treated royally. The Rawal gave him a big bag of prasad (blessed food), directly from the Abishekam and also the golden temple cloth itself.

Different from Kedarnath, Badrinath is accessible by car. It has a beautiful, majestically decorated entrance with a big bell. Down by the entrance were two natural very hot spring water ponds (Napta Kund) where we took purification baths before the puja.

"I was a 19-year old boy the first time I visited Badrinath," said Swamiji. "The Lord permits me to visit it again forty years later. Now I am a 60-year old man." He told us stories of his first pilgrimage, how he walked bare foot and without food on mountain trails, with the vow not to touch money, from Rishikesh to Badrinath.

"Narada, Sarada, Sri Sankaracharya, all of them have meditated here! They all came here!" exclaimed Swamiji with shining eyes while he was walking on the road bringing us down the hill.

Swamiji's own footprints are literally imprinted in these Himalayan regions. He stuck his feet on melted asphalt on the side of the road. It took time to remove the asphalt from his feet, even with gasoline! Later on, in the car, rushing down, he laughed wholeheartedly. "Sitaramananda! Tell everybody, you are the first disciple to do padapuja (ritual worship of the guru's feet) with petrol!"

Swami Sitaramananda

Swamiji always encouraged anyone who practiced a particular religion to stick with it. Priests, monks and rabbis were regular guests and speakers at the ashrams. The holidays of many different religions were honored and celebrated. He always said that the philosophy of yoga did not contradict the teachings of any religion and that practicing yoga would only enhance one's personal religious practices. At the same time he wouldn't hesitate to instruct students on the true meaning of the teachings of their own religion.

I had recently joined the *ashram* staff, and was working in Swamiji's house, setting up the Christmas tree. Swamiji was there in the room. I was still in awe of him, and felt nervous being with him in this casual way.

I was almost finished with my task when Swamiji said, "Jaya, fire proof the Christmas tree." I looked at the tree. The lights were all secure, and it was set up twenty feet from the fireplace. It seemed safe enough to me, so I just continued on with my work.

A few minutes later Swamiji again said, "Jaya, fireproof the Christmas tree!" This time he was a bit more emphatic. I looked at the tree and still couldn't see anything wrong. I told Swamiji that I thought it was fine the way it was. Then Swamiji, got more agitated. "No. No. Don't argue. Fireproof the Christmas tree!" he shouted.

I was getting very flustered. I didn't understand what he wanted. I pointed out that the wiring was all sound and that the tree was set up far away from the fireplace. He got even more agitated. "No! No! Jaya. You must spray it with that fireproofing spray. Fire proof the Christmas tree!!"

I didn't know anything about such a spray. I said, "Swamiji, I'm a Jew, what do I know about Christmas trees!" He replied, "I'm a Hindu, what do I know about Christmas trees!" Then we both laughed and I felt closer to him than I had felt before.

Jaya
Atlanta, Georgia

ॐ नमो नारायणाय

When Swamiji came to our home to meet my yoga students it was Passover, the Jewish holiday commemorating our freedom from slavery in Egypt. My heritage is important to me and my family, and Swamiji noticed our observances of this celebration. So that night he talked about the parting of the Red Sea when the Jews escaped and everyone in the pharaoh's army was drowned. "Do not be joyful that the Egyptians died," he admonished. "Do you think God loved them any less than you? They too were his children." As a Jew and as a yogi, he taught me to love my enemies, and to see each person as a messenger from God.

Sarabess Forster
Silver Springs, Maryland

Swamiji encouraged everyone, whether or not they belonged to a particular religious group, to pray. Prayer was a regular daily event at every *satsang*, and before and after every class.

One day, just as we were pulling out of the *ashram* gate in the car, Swamiji appeared on the path. We stopped to say good-bye. He told us to say the Om Trayambakam prayer three times every time we started the car. The prayer would give us protection during the trip. We of course immediately said the prayer with him, and then drove off.

Later on, as I reflected on this incident, I realized that Swamiji had been teaching us on more than one level. On the surface he genuinely believed that saying the prayer before we drove away would protect us on our journey. On a more subtle level he was helping us to always remember God. He had taken a mundane, everyday act like starting the car and spiritualized it.

Swamiji was always emphasizing the importance of ceaselessly remembering God, trying to keep God always in the mind. By associating a simple physical act like starting the car with remembering God he was helping us discipline the mind. Instead of just jumping in the car and rushing off, we would regularly take a few moments to pause and reflect.

The act he chose to associate with the thought wasn't that important. What he really accomplished was getting us to regularly stop and remember God. It could have been anything we normally did; get on a bus, turn on the stove, or even flush the toilet. Any act can be become a spiritual act. All you need to do is remember God as you do it.

Gopala Krishna

ॐ नमो नारायणाय

One particular recollection has left its mark and become more meaningful as time has passed. Swamiji asked me to help edit his book, *The Complete Illustrated Book of Yoga*. Before I could work on editing it, I had to make it clear in all honesty, that I didn't believe in God, that I had long since made my peace in the matter by deciding that I was God and, if I had anything to pray for, I had better pray to myself to do something about it. Swamiji's gentle "That's just what we yogis believe" has stayed with me and has taken years to ripen and bear fruit.

Sylvia K
New York, NY

I Am Not This Body

The following is an excerpt from a talk Swamiji gave in the mid-to-late 1980's in Berlin, hence all the references to Germany.

To understand yoga philosophy two things are important: all things are changing—you can't stop the process even for a moment—and matter will not be destroyed. These processes of change, you call birth and death. The death of the tomato in my mouth is the birth of my body; the death of my body is the birth of new worms or germs or bacteria or plants. Matter cannot be created or destroyed, but matter does not stay in the same state; it changes.

The body is changing at this very moment. Look carefully at my hair. Do you see any new gray hairs coming up? At this very moment do you see any new gray hairs? Or does my hair appear to stay exactly the same from moment to moment? Can this process of change be stopped at a certain time? If I put some Grecian Formula on my hair, is the process stopped? Whether you are seeing it or not, the process goes on. Look at the pictures in *The Complete Illustrated Book of Yoga*. These are all pictures of me when I was thirty; now I'm sixty. The body you see here with you, when I came from India, it was not like this. I see the difference in the body.

But this change does not take place over night, nor does it happen once a year. Does it happen? Suddenly your birthday comes and your body is one year older. How does that change takes place? Moment by moment. That process is not stopping; it has never stopped. If I come back here ten or fifteen years from now, my body will be different. But that change you are going to notice in ten or fifteen years is taking place even at this moment. But don't forget, you are also changing at the same time. You are thinking, "Well, of course, Swami Vishnu is getting old, but we are going to be young forever." You are also changing at this very moment. In another thirty of forty years you will see all the changes. This building is changing; the planet earth, the sun, the moon, and the stars, the galaxies - nothing stays in the same state even for a moment. That's the philosophy of yoga.

Change is inevitable. Can you find anything without change? Ah, now comes the answer only yoga can give. All objects, all matter, change, but the subject will never change. Now, what is the subject? The subject is "I am" and the object is anything which is not me. Whatever is not "I" must be object, you understand that? So I am? Subject. And you are all? Objects.

This flower, is it subject or object? An object, of course. What is the quality of objects, of matter? What is the quality of all things? All things change every moment and all objects can be handed over and also taken back. So all objects will change and are changing moment by moment, and all objects can be handed over or taken back. This is a standard law, a basic law, for objects. This cloth, is it subject or object? Even though I am wearing this cloth, still it won't be subject, will it? It is changing, isn't it? And I can give this cloth away. So obviously it is object. It is changing and it can be given.

But now the problem is this finger. Is it subject or object? Some people say it is subject. That's the problem in the West. So, this is an Indian finger, is it not? It's a Hindu finger too; it's also a swami's finger. So this subject is Hindu, Swami and Indian. But tomorrow my student tells me, "Swamiji, I'm working in Paris, and there's quite a lot of work for me, so I need one more finger." So we go to the doctor, and the doctor takes this finger and puts it on his hand. Now whose finger is it? Is it still my finger even though now it's on his hand? Whose finger is it? Who is using it? He is using it like it was his own finger. There's one quality of an object; you can hand it over or take it back.

The next question is, "Is this finger changing?" Just look at your finger. When you were a baby, it could bend all the way back. Now, it stays straight like a steel pipe, but your fingers were very flexible once upon a time. Then comes the arthritis, and the hand is stiff and bent. Have you seen people with arthritic hands? Those hands did not start out like that, and they didn't change all at once. It all takes place moment by moment. If you don't believe it, look at your hand after thirty years. It changes. So it can't be subject. If you don't agree with me, I've got another example.

On Saturday I felt some pain in my chest, in my heart. I rushed to the doctor. "Doctor! Doctor! My heart is attacking me!"

The doctor says, "O.K. Swamiji, I'm going to check everything for you. Hmm, yes. Your heart is attacking; I can see your attacking heart."

"What shall I do doctor?"

"Don't worry. I have a sharp knife. I'll cut your attacking heart out and throw it away. And I'll give you a monkey heart."

"Thank you Doctor. You are great."

So my sweet heart has gone into the dust bin and my new heart is a monkey heart. Now, with a monkey heart, who is the subject "I am"? Who am I? Will you hear my message when I've got a monkey heart? Won't you think a monkey is speaking to you? "Hey monkey! We don't want your monkey heart speaking to us like this." "He's a monkey!" Would you still give me precious gifts? Will you bring some flowers for me when I have a monkey heart? Be careful, because I've got a monkey heart, and monkeys eat up flowers. But the subject is still the same, is it not? "I am" is the same.

Well, if that is so, what about with the liver? "Doctor! Doctor! My liver is attacking me!"

The Doctor examined me, he took blood, and told me, "Swami Vishnu, you've got very little blood in your alcohol stream!"

"What shall I do Doctor?"

"I'll give you a pig's liver."

A man in America lived for fifteen days with a pig's liver (I'm not making up a story, really. He lived for fifteen days with a pig's liver.) On the next day I need a kidney because my kidneys have failed, and I get goat kidneys.

Next my blood is all poisoned. How many types of blood are there? Well, let's see. There's German blood, English blood, Russian, American, Hindu, and African blood, Protestant blood, East Berlin blood, West Berlin blood... How many types of blood are there? Four: A, B, AB, and O. You can find these four types anywhere in the world. My Hindu A blood is not good so the doctor says he can give a transfusion of new blood, but there is only one Hindu here and he's got B blood, "O Swami, I'm a Hindu. I'll give you my B blood."

Then someone else says, "No Swamiji, I've got A blood, German A blood."

"Oh No no no! I don't want German blood in my body. I'm an Indian Hindu. I will take only Hindu blood."

But when it is Hindu B blood I will die. The body won't care whether it is Hindu or American, as long as it's A blood from any source. So the doctor took all my Hindu A blood and gave me German A blood.

Now, I've got a monkey's heart, a pig's liver, goat's kidneys and German blood. "What about your religion Swamiji, and nationality?" Well, I was an Indian before, but for thirty years I've been living in Canada; I've got a Canadian passport; I travel as a Canadian. If this body had an Indian passport I wouldn't be able to come past the German border, even though the body is the same. The fact that they see an Indian passport—just the name Indian on a piece of paper—"Oh no! You need a visa. If I want to stay here one month, it will take me about three months to get a visa. With a Canadian passport, I just go through. So I'm Canadian. "And what about religion, Swamiji?" Well, I became a Swami, a Hindu monk. So the people can understand, it's like a priest, Father John. And what about sex? A little operation with hormones and I become a woman. This happens often.

So now, with a monkey-heart, pig's liver, goat's kidneys, German blood, with plastic nose and plastic eyes, Miss Father John. Who am I? Who am I? I am coming here. I have all these different parts; I have them in this body now, exactly as I have described, and I am talking to you. Who am I? Am I changed? Has my personality changed? I am that? I am that? I am that?

I Am That I Am. I am not Vishnu; I am not a Canadian; I'm not a German; I am not this body; I am not the hand, heart, liver, feet, kidneys; I am not the mind; I am not intellect; I am not the astral body; I am not the causal body; I Am. "I Am." That's the answer to Who Am I? That's the central philosophy of yoga, and the purpose of life is to find this I.

In January of 1991 Swamiji suffered a stroke that left him paralyzed on the left side of the body and with minimal speech. A few months later his kidneys failed and he needed to have daily dialysis treatments. For many years before this Swamiji had been telling us in *satsang*, "One day I will be old and crippled, sitting in a wheel chair, looking like this." Then he would slouch over and wrinkle up his face. We would all laugh. Surely he was just illustrating a point, that death would come to all of us some day.

It was like Swamiji had been preparing us for this time. Until his *mahasamadhi* in November, 1993 he had to have constant care and attention. Many of his students spent time taking care of him during this time. For all of them it was a object lesson in "I am not this body."

In the summer of 1991 I went to the *ashram* in Val Morin for two weeks. I was looking forward to helping out and doing some karma yoga. Since I was fairly handy, I figured I'd be put on the maintenance crew and take part in one of the usual summer construction projects. Much to my surprise, I was asked if I would do the "night shift", helping take care of Swamiji. I gladly accepted, little knowing what I was getting in to.

For most of the first week, Swamiji was in hospital in Montreal, where he was being treated for kidney failure. I would leave for the city around 6:00 PM, drive for an hour, and start my shift at 7:00 PM. I was there with one and sometimes two other staff members. We slept on the floor beside his bed, ready to do whatever Swamiji needed us to do. We seldom got much sleep.

Swamiji was in a great deal of pain and discomfort. Because he was paralyzed down his left side, he couldn't roll over, sit up, lie down, go to the toilet, or anything without our help. We were always massaging his legs and back, trying to ease the soreness and tightness. He didn't like the hospital food, and would be hungry at odd hours. We would often end up feeding him or giving him something to drink in the middle of the night. He was often restless, and we would have to help him out of bed and into the wheel chair, and then wheel him up and down the hospital corridors. Every time we moved him, we would have to put our arms around him and lift him up. We had to be careful not to bump the dialysis shunts sticking out of his neck.

It was wonderful. I hugged Swamiji many times every night. I loved just putting my arms around him, feeling him let me take control of his body for him. I knew that every time I moved him it hurt, but he never complained. Instead, as I lifted him, he would say "Ram."

Early in the morning, around 5:30 or so, before the daily activities of the hospital got under way, we would have our own little *satsang*, meditating and chanting softly, so as not to disturb the other people in the hospital. I always got a tremendous amount of energy from this private darshan, often just myself and Swami Kartikeyananda, sitting on opposite sides of the bed, and Swamiji lying or half sitting on the bed.

Around 7:00 AM the "day shift" would come in and I would drive back to the *ashram*, arriving around 8:00. I'd report in to the senior staff, and then crawl into my tent to sleep for a few hours, until brunch at 10:00 AM. After brunch the tent was too hot, so I'd curl up in a blanket and do my best to sleep on the grass under a tree in the midst of the busy *ashram*, with people coming and going and bells ringing. I'd get up around 2:00 PM, go for a swim and a sauna, do some asanas and pranayama, eat a quick dinner, and drive back to Montreal for the next shift.

I was probably getting at most four hours sleep a day, and that was always broken up into small chunks and naps. What was amazing to me was that I felt incredible. Often I would finish my shift and have trouble going to sleep because I was so energized from being with Swamiji. I often wondered who was taking care of whom. It became clear to me that I may have been serving Swamiji's body, but he was taking care of me, giving me the energy I needed to carry on.

I remember one sunny morning, after finishing my shift, standing talking to several other people. I was really high, full of energy. I was excited too. I said to the others, "He's not that body! It's really clear to me that his body has nothing to do with who he really is." They all just smiled. Despite his own pain and discomfort, Swamiji was using his physical condition as just another way to teach me the lessons I needed to learn. I finally understood in a concrete way what Swamiji had been saying all those years.

Gopala Krishna

In October 1992 Swamiji undertook a *Ganga parigrama,* a pilgrimage down the sacred Ganges River in India, from its source at Gomukh in the Himalayas to its mouth in Calcutta.

On the day we left Gangotri, Swamiji had a very difficult trip down the mountains, with much vomiting and diarrhea. After one particularly distressing bout, we stopped the van to clean him up. Swami Kartikeyananda, Gayatri and Prahlad were at Swamiji's feet, attempting to change his soiled dhoti and sheets. I was very gingerly lifting his head, frightened of the pain from his recently broken vertebrae. As I lifted his head and tried to sponge some of the mess from his hair Swamiji looked at me and said, "Kamala, are you all right?" I stared at this poor, broken body covered in such a mess and said "Yes Swamiji, I'm fine." I looked down at the others, all falling about with laughter. They were used to Swamiji's ways. He was asking me about a migraine I had suffered five days before, completely oblivious to his own distress.

Kamala
Katomba, Australia

Swamiji's *guru*, Swami Sivananda, also had trouble with his legs late in his life. For long periods of time he couldn't walk at all, except by exerting great willpower. One example of this was during the first Parliament of Religions, organized by Sivananda in the 1950's. It was a gathering of religious leaders from many different faiths, demonstrating the unity of all religions. Swamiji remembered it well:

It was during the Parliament of Religions, the first one. It was the very biggest celebration, that Parliament of Religions; all the great leaders from various countries came for this function and Master was the great host who invited all these great people from all over, from Japan and other places. Master had lumbago and arthritis. Just a few days before the inauguration day, during the intense preparations, Master had terrible lumbago. He could not even move from the bed. Doctors said that he wouldn't be able to get up for several months. Master could not get up, but he still followed his strict routine. At a certain time he would do a certain thing; when the time came for writing his book every day, he would spend the time writing. Now he could not get up and write so he wrote lying down, but still he kept up his routine.

We were all worried because without him that whole Parliament of Religions wouldn't be anything. His presence was necessary, but he could not even move. Many Ministers and great politicians began arriving. Master was supposed to give the welcome address at the inauguration. But how could he do that? Master's cottage was at the very bottom of a big hill, near the Ganges. At the very top of that hill was the main *ashram* and the yoga hall where all the big functions take place. That meant he had to walk up from the bottom, from the Ganges, to the top of the hill. But he could not even move his back; he had been lying in bed for several days and doctors said he would not be able to move for a very long time.

Then, just half an hour before the function was to begin, he just got up from the bed and walked up the hill. Exactly on time he stood and delivered his welcome address. He spoke standing for more than an hour, and then he walked back down the hill and got back into bed. He couldn't move afterwards. You see, he did not just remove the pain whenever he wanted. Sages can conquer the pain if they want, but only at the crucial time did he use his will power to overcome the pain. For several months afterwards he just lay in bed. This is called *prarabdha karma,* that karma which we must experience in this lifetime. Even sages and saints won't try to avoid it because the purpose of this body is to undergo that *karma.*

Even though he was paralyzed on his left side and had severe problems with his right leg as well, Swami Vishnu-devananda would also exert himself when it was necessary, in some ways reflecting the story he told about Sivananda.

In April of 1991 I was asked to help take care of Swamiji for a month. My heart was heavy, because I did not know in what condition I would find him. I had known Swamiji for twenty-five years, since I was fifteen. He was a man without limitations, full of love, creativity and a profound respect for humanity. How could he express himself now without the ability to talk, to walk, to do asanas, to fly, with all his movements curtailed?

My big surprise was that Swamiji didn't miss his body. I was now in the presence of a wiser, more saintly Swamiji—full of sweetness, peace, and love. He always joked about his condition, saying "I am not this body, this body is not me." I never once heard him complain about his condition. He did pray and meditate more and he never, for one moment, ceased to serve and be involved with all that was happening around him.

When I was alone on night shift I was afraid I'd drop off to sleep, or that I'd not be able to understand his slurred speech, or not know what to do. It was a bit like caring for a baby. I've had babies, but I'd never taken care of a sick Swamiji; he had always taken care of me.

One night a thick fog came up, reducing visibility to practically zero. Swamiji nonetheless wanted to go for his usual late night drive. I called the main office and Hanuman (a disciple who lived near the *ashram* and often helped with Swamiji) but no one answered the phone. I approached Swamiji and gently told him that the staff must be very tired and that it would be quite dangerous to go out in this weather. Swamiji said OK.

Ten minutes later he again requested a drive in the car. I phoned everyone again, with the same results. This time Swamiji said, "OK, prepare a bath." This would also be a big problem for me. Swamiji was downstairs. I knew it would be impossible to bring him upstairs to the bathroom single-handed.

Nevertheless I said "Yes Swamiji." I went upstairs, prepared the bath, and when all was ready, Swamiji told me to wake up Swami Kartikeyananda. I went to her room, and asked her for help with Swamiji. She was too tired to answer me, let alone get up.

This was the first time I didn't go rushing to Swamiji's call. But I couldn't bring myself to refuse him, so I just pushed myself on. He took my arm and very slowly we headed for the stairs. All I could think of was praying for success. Swamiji made an enormous effort to move his legs, but could not, so and asked me for assistance. I don't know how long it took, but we finally reached the bathroom at the top of the stairs. He lay in the bathtub for a very long time.

Kanti Devi
Montevideo, Uruguay

ॐ नमो नारायणाय

I met Swamiji while doing teacher training in Canada in 1991. I knew beforehand that he was suffering a painful disease which forced him to be in a wheelchair. On the first evening of the course it was rumored that Swamiji would come to the yoga hall. All the students felt excited at the possibility of seeing Swamiji; I myself had never seen him.

When he arrived I saw a man, clearly an Indian figure, walking on his own two legs! Two men were helping him every moment with great care. Swamiji made some gesture to them, indicating to them that they needn't be so attentive.

My first impression of Swamiji was very powerful. He appeared "wild", like a lion, incredibly physically strong—a person quite out of the ordinary. Never had I felt such an emotion. I cried as I have never before cried in my life. What this fierce man taught me was to have courage and persevere to the very end.

Brahmaswaroop
Madrid, Spain

Swamiji in 1992.

Completion

In the last few years of his life Swamiji took on one more great task, the building of a new temple at the Val Morin *Ashram,* dedicated to Subramanya and Ayyappa. Subramanya was Swamiji's family deity. Ayyappa is a deity worshipped in South India. Tradition has it that Ayyappa's greatest devotee, Vavar, was a Muslim. This was significant to Swamiji, who spoke out constantly against Hindu-Muslim violence in India.

Why was it so important to build this temple? This is what Swamiji said.

> Without devotion, without God's grace, all our efforts are meaningless. We cannot reach the top. No matter how much we strive, *maya* will overpower and push us down. Devotion is very important in the spiritual path. God's grace must be there.

Like many of Swamiji's projects, the temple started as a thought in his mind. He then focused all his energy on making that thought manifest. One of his students remembers how it all started.

> In July of 1992 I was on staff at the *ashram* in Val Morin. I was lucky enough to be down at Swamiji's house. We were carrying him to sites around the house, doing a small pilgrimage, chanting and offering flowers. Out of the blue Swamiji said he wanted to go on a bigger pilgrimage up the hill behind the ashram we called Mount Kailas to pick a site for a new temple. Swami Kartikeyananda asked him how we were going to get him up the hill since there was no trail and the ashram was at the very bottom of the hill. Swamiji persisted.
>
> Sure enough we pulled him up the mountain in his wheel chair, all of us chanting *mantras.* It was unbearable pulling him up there. He was heavy. We were grabbing each side of the wheel chair and hauling him up. There were mosquitoes everywhere and we were all being bitten, and trying to make sure that Swamiji wasn't bitten. The funny thing was that at the time no one seemed to care about the difficulties. It was really hot and we were all sweating, but anything Swamiji wanted we of course did.
>
> When we got to the top of the hill we were surrounded by trees. He picked a site for the temple, it was just a rock in the woods. We placed a *kaavadi* we had carried up with us and flowers we had picked along the way on the rock. I felt really exhilarated.
>
> When I heard there really was going to be a temple there I immediately thought of the small (10 feet square) Siva temple on the hill at the Yoga Ranch

in Woodbourne. The following year when I returned here the site had been cleared and the rock had been laid bare. There were statues of the two deities, Subramanya and Ayappa, and an Indian canopy. It was very peaceful. Already devotees were doing *pujas*, raising up the energy. Now, two years later, there is a huge temple up there. It's quite beautiful and people are coming from all over to worship. When we carried Swamiji up the hill I didn't know that it was going to be what it has turned out to be today. I feel really honored to have been a part of it.

Uma
Chicago, Illinois

Throughout the summer of 1993, Swamiji's health deteriorated. He seldom used a wheel chair. Instead he was carried everywhere on a stretcher. He focused all of his energy on getting the temple built.

Several times, in September and October, Swamiji had Swami Kartikeyananda book tickets to India. Then he would cancel the trip. He seemed torn between completing his *karma*—the construction of the temple—and his desire to be in India when he left his body. Finally, early in the morning on October 17th, each of the members of the Executive Board, Swamiji's senior disciples, received a call. "Swamiji wants you to come right away." Each of us, as we flew from our respective places, thought that Swamiji was leaving his body. When we arrived, however, Swamiji seemed strong and vibrant. He conveyed to each of us the importance of the temple, as a physical manifestation of his life's work. We realized that this was Swamiji's last wish. Each of us made a promise that the temple would be completed.

It seemed that only then did Swamiji feel that his last burden had been lifted. He left for India on October 22nd.

Swami Sankarananda

The temple, a beautiful 18 meter square building, was completed in the summer of 1994. The deities were installed on July 10th.

Once Swamiji arrived in India, he started off on a pilgrimage. His first stop was to be the Mookambika Devi Temple in Kollur, South India, where he had been many times before to commune with the Divine Mother. By the time he arrived at the temple, late on November 1st, his physical condition had deteriorated to such a degree that he was taken to a hospital in nearby Manipal the next day. He continued to get worse, and by the 4th he was in intensive care and on a respirator. Though he was in a great deal of discomfort, he seemed very detached and peaceful. By the morning of November 9th he had lost consciousness. The doctors turned off the respirators, and his body stopped breathing, according to the death certificate, at 12:28 PM.

Swamiji always said that when he was gone his body should be put into the Ganges near his small *Ashram* just outside Uttar Kashi, in Northern India. His wishes were carried out. Swami Sankarananda describes the day of Swamiji's *jalasamadhi*.

At the Sivananda Yoga Vedanta Nataraja Center in New Delhi, Swamiji's body lay in a very simple plywood casket just big enough for him. The mantra *Om Namah Sivaya* was handwritten in blue paint on the lid, and the word TOP showed where his head was. The Indian Airlines cargo stickers were still pasted to the sides. Swamiji had arrived in New Delhi by air from South India where he had taken Mahasamadhi.

The casket with Swamiji's body was in the large room on the ground floor of Uma Sharma's Dance School and the staff members of the Delhi center, located on the top floor, were sitting at his feet. It was very early in the morning on Thursday, the 11th of November. Thursday is Guru's day, and so this was a good day for Jala Samadhi, the immersion of Swamiji's body in Mother Ganga, as per his wishes. Moreover, this particular Thursday was the day on which Lord Krishna, in his *lila* as the divine cowherd, brings the cows 'home from the forest.'

The lid was opened for a short period so that those present could view Swamiji, shrouded in a white cloth, except for his face. His beard had been shaven in the hospital and he had that peaceful smile that he always had when everything was well. We prostrated, offered flowers and touched his feet, closed and locked the casket and sat down to chant.

At exactly 4:00 AM a small party set out from New Delhi to make the journey to Uttar Kashi, to the Sivananda Kutir *Ashram* on the banks of the Ganges at Nettala, just 10 kilometers north of Uttar Kashi on the Gangotri road. There Swamiji had established an *Ashram* in his last days and had repeatedly said that when he left His body we should "throw it in the Ganga" there. His wishes were being fulfilled in that same subtle and strange manner that all his thoughts and actions were.

Chanting the same mantras that were always chanted whenever Swamiji went on a pilgrimage around his headquarters at the Yoga Camp, we gently loaded the casket into a small ambulance. Swami Hariomananda and Prahlad climbed in next to the casket to hold it securely on the long bumpy journey ahead. Potti Swami, a brahmin priest, who had come up from Trivandrum in South India immediately upon hearing of Swamiji's Mahasamadhi, got in the front seat. The rest of the party boarded a bus.

The early morning ride was quite pleasant and everyone dozed off, being in various states of travel lag. Before long the Ganga at Haridwar came into view and at about 9:30 AM we were winding through the bustling streets of Rishikesh, headed for the Sivananda's *ashram* outside Rishikesh where Swamiji could once again take permission from Master Sivananda for the journey to the Himalayan regions.

A huge reception was awaiting Swamiji. A carpet and a long, wide yellow canopy covered a 50-yard stretch of the road along the Ganga near Master's Kutir. Swami Adhyatmananda of the Divine Life Society was directing the ambulance to back up along this covered section of road, lined on both sides with hundreds upon hundreds of Swamis and others who came to pay their respects and receive Swamiji's blessings.

The casket was gently removed from the ambulance and laid on a bench in the middle of the road, where it was immediately surrounded by the large crowd. The lid was opened and people pressed forward to garland Swamiji with mala after mala of large orange and yellow marigolds. A path was made for Swami Krishnananda, a senior disciple of Swami Sivananda, and a contemporary of Swamiji's from his days in Rishikesh. In a strong sweet voice, he gave a moving talk in praise of Swamiji, his dedication to Master Sivananda and his work. He said that Swamiji was a true *sannyasi*, owning nothing. A fax from Swami Chidananda, the director of the *ashram*, was read and then *arati* was done. The casket, closed again, was placed in the ambulance and we set off on the last leg of the journey to Nettala. Two more cars, with ten Swamis from the Divine Life Society headed by Swami Adhyatmananda, accompanied us.

The kitchen of The Divine Life Society prepared food which was brought along on the journey. After an hour we stopped alongside the road for a quick meal and tea. It was important to reach Uttar Kashi before evening and the long windy road through the Garwhal Himalayas still lay ahead. After the junction at Tehri the road travels alongside the Ganga, here known as Bhagirathi. It was an incredibly clear blue day (often it is smoky and hazy in the afternoon) and we had a constant beautiful view of Mother Ganga, that stream of consciousness on earth through which Master had given Swamiji his first glimpse of the Infinite so many years ago, and to which Swamiji was now returning on this sacred day when Krishna brings the cows home.

Sensing the urgency, or being pushed by Swamiji's will, the drivers of the vehicles were speeding towards the destination. Already the sun was settling behind the tall peaks and the peaceful atmosphere of dusk could be felt. We halted briefly in Uttar Kashi to inform Swami Chaitanyananda of our arrival, but were told that he was already waiting at Nettala. Passing Swami Premananda's kutir, we saw him waiting and waved to him to come. As we approached the road down to the *ashram*, the sense of convergence to a point was becoming alarmingly powerful. Swamis, sadhus, and villagers were making their way resolutely towards the Ganga at the *ashram*.

The ambulance drove down, around the suspension bridge and backed up towards Swamiji's *kutir*. Swamiji was carried into the *kutir* and laid on a bed in the central room. A jeep with a large sturdy wooden casket was waiting . It had been prepared by the Swamis of the area in Swamiji's honor. The wood was good and there were gaps between the boards for the water to enter. Two caskets had been prepared; one in case Swamiji was in a sitting position, the other in case he was lying down. The latter was chosen and Swami Chaitanyananda and Swami Umananda from Kailas *ashram* directed the younger swamis to carry this beautiful casket to a high rock outcrop that juts into a curve of the Ganga where the water forms a large, calm and deep pool.

People were flowing in from everywhere and the intensity was mounting at a rapid rate. Inside the kutir, in Swamiji's room, Potti Swami began by asking Master Sivananda for permission to proceed to the Ganga. Harihara Chaitanya began ringing a bell.

God took over. Nothing more was said or asked of anybody. Chanting and the sound of bell and conch filled the air. The casket was lifted and Swamiji was carried in procession from the kutir to the Ganga. The energy was indescribable. Wonderment, mystery, calm and power, silence and noise, light and twilight and dark, clarity and confusion, joy and sorrow, ritual and avoidance of ritual—everything was present. Everything was exactly prepared and was taking place according to a divine script that only God knew. It was the *jala samadhi* of a true yogi.

A crowd of about 400 had massed on the smooth rock outcrop. The new casket was waiting on the highest point right at the edge of a five-foot drop into the Ganga . Swamiji was carried to a rock shelf just below this, removed from the old casket, and laid on his back on the rock. The timing was perfect. Had we arrived half an hour later it would have been missed.

Now everything seemed to be happening simultaneously: various swamis chanting different mantras and slokas, huge hand-held bunches of incense waving, bells ringing and the conch sounding again and again. The many garlands were removed by many hands and thrown into the Ganga, the cloths were taken from Swamiji and thrown into the Ganga. There he lay, naked on the rock, his face calm, his smile sweet and full, perhaps peeking from just under his eyelids. His arms lay alongside his body, palms down. Humility and magnificence were present together.

Then began the bathing with milk and Ganga water. Everyone around the body was bathing Swamiji. There was jostling as this and that Himalayan *mahatma* pressed his way through to bathe Swamiji with milk poured from a conch. Potti Swami made sure that all the senior disciples and staff present were able to do so also. Hands began passing beautiful new clean clothes - orange, red, yellow and white - and hands began wrapping Swamiji from head to foot, completely covering him. Garlands were placed around his neck, on his chest, at his feet, everywhere. Everything was happening with such an energy and intensity that it felt like this was the center of the vortex of the universe, a convergence of beings radiating out into infinity, Swamiji at the very center.

Swamiji's body, completely shrouded and garlanded, was gently raised and brought to the new casket, waiting on the higher rock shelf. Thick new ropes were draped over the sides and a few blankets were laid on top of the ropes . Then Swamiji was lowered into the casket and covered with more woolen blankets. The ropes were tied over the top of his body and again the many hands started passing large heavy rocks to lower into the casket around the body. All this while, *arati* was being done, boxes of burning incense were being waved around Swamiji, young Himalayan sadhus with powerful voices were calling to Mother Ganga and the high Himalayas. The elder and respected Swamis of the region were doing everything themselves. With a profound dignity, they began to hammer the lid of the casket closed, their eyes twinkling and blazing.

It was now nearly dark. A Petromax lamp was giving light. People cleared away from the side of the casket next to the Ganga and gathered on the other side. All pushed the now extremely heavy casket to the edge. An expectant calm descended. The previous chaotic intensity became quiet and united as the casket moved little by little to the very edge of the rock where it rested leaning slightly towards the Ganga. A moment passed for everyone to become clear and ready. Time was still.

Bolo Sat *Guru* Sivananda Maharaja Ki - JAI

Bolo Swami Vishnu-devananda Maharaja Ki - JAI
Gangayai Himalaya Bhagavan Ki - JAI

The voices of all rose into the dark twilight. At the precise destined moment, exactly according to Swamiji's wishes, exactly according to his ever-present will, the jala samadhi took place. The casket majestically moved off the edge, splashed into Mother Ganga, and remained still with the head tilted upwards, a good sign it was said, just another wink from Swamiji. For a long moment it remained there, and then two long bamboo poles nudged it down till it slipped below the surface. The poles fell into the Ganga and formed a cross above the spot. It was 5:40 in the evening.

A huge cheer arose. Then everyone abruptly turned and in a moment were gone.

The next day the flower garlands which had been thrown into the Ganga were still in the same place, kept in a small back eddy. And there they remained for days, freshly blooming in the Ganga waters.

On the rock where Swamiji lay naked a small shrine will be built.

OM TAT SAT

Sadhana Tattwa

In the opening chapter, Swamiji talks about a pamphlet that he found in a garbage can in his office. The contents of this pamphlet were his first glimpse of spiritual life. It drove him to meet Swami Sivananda, his future *guru*.

What was it about this little pamphlet that so enthralled the young man? It is probably best to let the words speak for themselves.

The Science of Seven Cultures
for Quick Evolution of the Human Soul
by
H. H. Sri Swami Sivananda

An ounce of practice is worth tons of theory. Practice yoga, religion and philosophy and attain self-realization.

These thirty-two instructions give the essence of the eternal religion *(Sanatana Dharma)* in its purest form. They are suitable for modern busy householders with fixed hours of work. Modify them to suit your convenience and increase the period gradually.

In the beginning take only a few practicable resolves which form a small but definite advance over your present habits and character. In case of ill-health, pressure of work, or unavoidable engagements, replace your active *sadhana* by frequent remembering of God.

Health Culture

Eat moderately. Take light and simple food. Offer it to God before you eat. Have a balanced diet.

Avoid chilies, garlic, onions, tamarind, etc., as far as possible. Give up tea, coffee, smoking, betels, meat and wine entirely.

Fast on *ekadasi* days (once a fortnight). Take milk, fruit and roots only. Practice yogic asanas or physical exercise for fifteen to thirty minutes. Take a long walk or play some vigorous game daily.

Energy Culture

Observe silence for two hours daily and four to eight hours on Sundays.

Observe celibacy according to your age and circumstances. Restrict the indulgence to once a month. Decrease it gradually to once a year. Finally take a vow of abstinence for life.

Ethical Culture

Speak the truth. Speak little. Speak kindly. Speak sweetly.
Do not injure anyone in thought, word or deed. Be kind to all.
Be sincere, straightforward and open-hearted in all your talks and dealings.
Be honest. Earn by the sweat of your brow. Do not accept any money, present or favor unless earned lawfully.
Develop nobility and integrity.
Control fits of anger by developing serenity, patience, love, mercy and tolerance. Forget and forgive. Adapt yourself to men and events.

Will Culture

Live without sugar for a week or month. Give up salt on Sundays.
Give up playing cards, reading novels, and visiting the cinema and club. Fly from evil company. Avoid discussions with materialists. Do not mix with persons who have no faith in God or who criticize your *sadhana.*
Curtail your wants. Reduce your possessions. Have plain living and high thinking.

Heart Culture

Doing good to others is the highest religion. Do some selfless service for a few hours every week, without egoism or expectation of reward. Do your worldly duties in the same spirit. Work is worship. Dedicate it to God.
Give two to ten percent of your income to charity every month. Share what you have with others. Let the world be your family. Remove selfishness.
Be humble and prostrate to all beings mentally. Feel the divine presence everywhere. Give up vanity, pride and hypocrisy.
Have unwavering faith in God, Gita and your *guru.* Make a total self-surrender to God and pray: "Thy will be done, I want nothing." Submit to the divine will in all events and happenings with equanimity.
See God in all beings and love them as your own self. Do not hate anyone.
Remember God at all times or at least on rising from bed, during a pause in work, and before going to bed. Keep a *japa mala* (rosary) in your pocket.

Psychic Culture

Study one chapter or ten to twenty-five verses of the *Gita,* with meaning, daily. Learn Sanskrit, at least sufficient to understand the *Gita* in the original.
Memorize the whole *Gita* gradually. Keep it always at your side.
Read *Ramayana, Bhagavata, Upanishads, Yoga Vasishtha* or other religious books daily or on holidays.
Attend religious meetings, *kirtans* and *satsangs* of saints at every opportunity. Organize such functions on Sundays and holidays.
Visit a temple or a place of worship at least once a week and arrange to hold *kirtans* or discourses there.

Spend your holidays and leave periods, when possible, in the company of saints, or practice *sadhana* at holy places in seclusion.

Spiritual Culture

Go to bed early. Get up at 4 A.M. Answer calls of nature, clean your mouth and take a bath.

Recite some prayers and *kirtan dwanis*. Practice *pranayama, japa* and meditation from 5 A.M. to 6 A.M. Sit in *padmasana, siddhasana* or *sukhasana* throughout the sitting, without any movement.

Perform your daily *sandhya, gayatri japa, nityakarma* and worship, if any.

Write your favorite *mantra* or name of God in a notebook for ten to thirty minutes daily.

Sing the names of the Lord *(kirtan)*. Repeat some prayers, *stotras* and *bhajans* for half to one hour at night, together with your family and servants.

Make annual resolves on the above lines. Regularity, tenacity and fixity are essential. Record your sadhana in a spiritual diary daily. Review it every month and correct failures.

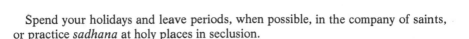

The practical words of advice in this document were always close to Swamiji's heart and formed the cornerstone of how he taught and acted for the rest of his life. In particular, the opening sentence, "An ounce of practice is worth tons of theory," succinctly describes his approach to the philosophy of yoga. Don't just talk about it, do it now.

To make it easier to act, Swamiji encouraged his students to follow the other main piece of advice found in the introduction, "take only a few practicable resolves which for a small but definite advance over your present habits and character." Every New Year's Eve he would encourage his students to make a set of resolutions for the coming year, based on the thirty-two points found in Sadhana Tattwa. Here is how he explained the process.

> When I was in the Himalayas undergoing my own training, I kept a resolve form according to Gurudev's instructions There was a diary to see that resolves were kept properly and that the technique was being followed. One noted daily: how many hours asanas were done, how many rounds of pranayama, how many hours of silence, how many times the temper was lost, how many times one failed in brahmacharya. Then at evening one checked the diary and compared it with the resolve form so on the next day one could renew the effort to do even better.
>
> After several days of failure, suddenly one is able to reach his goal. Then one would increase the resolve to a higher level. Instead of doing pranayama only twice a day, one does it three

times daily. The spiritual diary shows whether one is progressing or not. It is very important for every spiritual aspirant to be able to see his own progress. It will become a kind of guide or teacher to watch over his shoulder.

You all make resolutions at New Years do you not? You resolve not to smoke, not to eat meat, not to drink alcohol, or not to smoke marijuana. However, if you are 100% successful, then it is not a proper resolve because it is already your way of life. You must take something that you are still imperfect at and wish to improve. If I were to take the above four resolves, I would be completely successful in them, so instead I should take a useful resolve such as, "I will not get angry." Every year I fail in this resolve, so I modify it. Instead of getting angry every second day, I will get angry every third day.

I no longer keep a written spiritual diary, but I do continue to keep one in my brain. Before I go to bed I examine how many times I got angry or how many times I shouted. Then I pray to God and say, "Oh Lord, I am offering this to you." In this way I surrender. That is what resolves are all about.

Do not make a resolve you cannot follow to a certain extent because if you put too many resolves in the beginning, it is like putting overload on a weak muscle. It will collapse. Discipline should be slow and gradual to avoid having the mind rebel. Make realistic resolves, and then look in your diary. Perhaps you resolved to get up at 5 A.M. If on twenty days of the month you got up at 8 A.M. and on ten days you were able to get up at 5 A.M., then you are happy. Perhaps on twenty days you performed only one hour of asanas, but on ten days you did two hours of asanas. Perhaps on twenty days you did only five rounds of pranayama, but on ten days you were able to do forty rounds.

At the end of each month, study your performance and decide how to improve even further. At the end of a year you will find that your will power has increased tremendously. Then you will know that you are a free man, that you made your mind do your bidding. After five or six years of such practice, you will find that meditation will come naturally. The moment you sit, energy will move, all the *chakras* will be blossoming, and your face will be shining and radiant.

Glossary

anuloma viloma   The practice of alternate nostril breathing.

arati   A prayer in which a flame is offered to God in all his/her forms. The flame is waved before the images on the altar and then offered to all those in attendance. Normally camphor is burned, because it leaves no trace after it is completely burned. This symbolizes the removal of our ego.

asana   Literally, "still posture." The asanas are the poses used in hatha yoga.

ashram   A place of spiritual retreat.

atman   The individual soul.

bandhas   Muscular locks applied to retain energy or prana while practicing hatha yoga.

Bhagavatam   The *Srimad Bhagavatam,* a Hindu scripture dealing with the life and teachings of Krishna.

bhakti   Devotion

biksha   Alms

brahmacharya   Celibacy, or more broadly, control of the senses. Also the name of the first step taken towards becoming a sanyasin, similar to a novice, monk, or nun in the Christian tradition.

Brahman   God. The absolute, indivisible energy of the universe.

chai   Indian tea, made by boiling water, milk, tea, and sugar together in a large pot, often over an open fire.

chakras   Astral energy centers or plexuses. Located along the spine, the chakras are storage places for prana.

chapatti	An Indian flat bread.
dakshina	An offering given to a guru when he/she gives mantra initiation to a student. Also an offering to a priest for performing a ritual or an artist for their performance.
darshan	The experience of being with a great saint, as in "having darshan of the guru." Also used in the context of experiencing oneness with God in some form, as in "having darshan of Lord Krishna."
devi	Goddess.
dharana	Concentration.
dhyana	Meditation.
Durga	The Divine Mother.
Ganga	The Ganges River; also the Goddess in the form of the river.
ghats	Built-up area on the edge of a river or pond used for bathing, with steps going down into the water.
gopi	A young woman, usually a milk maiden, from the Sanskrit word go, meaning "cow." Often used in reference to young women devoted to Krishna as described in the *Srimad Bhagavatam*.
guha	A cave.
hatha yoga	*Ha* literally means "sun" and *tha* means "moon." The yoga that brings about the balance of opposites. A practical way to control the mind through control of the prana.
jalasamadhi	Immersion of the body of a great soul in the Ganges.
kaavadi	A dome-shaped sculpture, with peacock feathers representing Lord Krishna, used in worship.
karma	Action operating through the law of cause and effect.
kapalabhatti	A breathing exercise used to oxygenate the blood and energize the body.
kirtan	Singing the Lord's name.

Krishna	An incarnation of the Vishnu. In the Hindu trinity, Vishnu is the preservative power of God. From time to time Vishnu incarnates on earth to bring the world back to righteousness. The principal character in the *Mahabharata* and the *Srimad Bhagavatam.*
kundalini	The primordial energy that lies dormant in the lowest chakra at the base of the spine. The practice of yoga awakens this energy.
kutir	Cottage, hut.
lila	The play of God in the world.
mahasamadhi	Final emancipation from the body and absorption in the Lord. Absorption of the individual consciousness into the cosmic consciousness.
mahatma	Great soul.
mala	A string of prayer beads.
mantra	God in the form of sound. A mystical or divine energy encased in a sound structure; Sanskrit word(s) repeated while meditating.
maya	The illusory power of the Lord. Maya makes us believe that impermanent things (e.g., the body) are permanent.
mouna	Silence. Also the observance of a vow of silence.
niyama	Ethical observances: purity, contentment, austerity, scriptural study, and surrender to God. Along with *yama, niyama* is the ethical foundation of raja yoga.
Om tat sat	A benediction; a solemn invocation of the divine blessing.
ojas	Life force, spiritual energy.
pada puja	*Pada* literally means "feet" and *puja* means "worship." A ceremony where the guru's feet are worshipped.
prana	Energy, life force.
pranam	The act of showing respect to another by bowing the

head with hands held on the chest in prayer position.

pranayama	The science of the control of the vital energy of life force, accomplished through breath control.
prasad	Blessed food given to the people at the end of a puja or satsang.
pratyahara	Withdrawal of the senses, or abstraction of the senses from objects. A step in the preparation for meditation.
puja	Worship ceremony.
pujari	One who participates in or leads a worship ceremony.
raja yoga	Yogic philosophy based on control of the mind as explained by Patanjali in the Raja Yoga Sutras. Also called ashtanga yoga, the yoga of eight limbs: yama, niyama, asana, pranayama, pratyahara, dharana, dhyana, samadhi.
Rama	The ideal householder, an incarnation of Vishnu.
rishi	A wise person, a teacher.
sadhana	Spiritual practice.
sadhu	A spiritual person, a practitioner of yoga.
saguna	With quality or attributes.
samadhi	The superconscious state. God-realization.
samsara	The round of births and deaths.
Samskaras	Impressions in the subconscious mind from previous experiences in this life or in past lives.
sanyasin	One who has renounced the world. A monk or nun. A sanyasin takes the three great vows of saucha (purity), bhiksha (living on alms), and dhyana (meditation).
satsang	Company of the wise or holy. A time when students gather around the teacher or together for group meditation and worship. From *sat,* meaning "wisdom or knowledge" and *sang,* meaning "gathering."
shakti	The female, creative force of the universe. Also Shakti,

God in female form.

Siva

In the Hindu trinity Siva is the destructive aspect of God. In this sense, destruction is good, implying destruction of the negative aspects of the self, making room for the positive aspects to grow and blossom.

Sivalingam

A stone or wooden phallus, representing Siva.

sloka

A verse of scripture.

swami

A sanyasin or renunciate.

untouchables

Outcasts. People who do not belong to any of the four Hindu castes. People of very low social status.

Vedanta

Literally "the end of the Vedas," the summation or end point of the philosophy of the *Vedas,* ancient Hindu scriptures. Often called *advaita vedanta,* the philosophy of non-dualism, as taught by Sri Sankaracharya.

yama

Ethical restrictions or self-restraints: non-injury, truth, celibacy, non-stealing, and non-covetousness. Along with *niyama, yama* forms the ethical basis of raja yoga.

yoga

Literally, "union." The union of the individual soul with the supreme soul, or God. The philosophical system and practices that lead to this union.

Resources

CANADA

Sivananda Yoga Vedanta Centre
77 Harbord Street
Toronto, Ontario M5S 1G4

Centre Sivananda de Yoga Vedanta
5178 Boul. St. Laurent
Montreal,Quebec H2T 1R8

Sivananda Ashram Yoga Camp
Eighth Avenue
Val Morin, Quebec J0T 2R0

USA

Sivananda Yoga Vedanta Center
243 W. 24th Street
New York, NY 10011

Sivananda Yoga Vedanta Center
1746 Abbot Kinney
Los Angeles, CA 90291

Sivananda Yoga Vedanta Center
1246 West Bryn Mawr
Chicago, IL 60660

Sivananda Yoga Vedanta Center
1200 Arguello Blvd.
San Francisco, CA 94122

Sivananda Ashram Yoga Ranch
P.O. Box 195
Woodbourne, NY 12788

Sivananda Ashram Yoga Farm
14651 Ballantree Lane Comp. 8
Grass Valley, CA 95949

EUROPE

Sivananda Yoga Vedanta Zentrum
Rechte Weinzeile 29-3-9
Vienna 1040, Austria

Sivananda Yoga Vedanta Centre
51 Felsham Road
London SW15 1AZ, England

Centre Sivananda de Yoga Vedanta
123 Boul. de Sebastopol
Paris 75002, France

Sivananda Yoga Vedanta Centre
Heilbronnestr. 21
1 Berlin 30 - 10779, Germany

Sivananda Yoga Vedanta Zentrum
Steinheilst 1, 8
Munish - 80333, West Germany 2

Centro de Yoga Sivananda Vedanta
Juan Bravo 62, 7A
Madrid 28006, Spain

Centre Sivananda de Yoga Vedanta
1 rue des Minoteries
Geneve 1205, Switzerland

ISRAEL

Sivananda Yoga Vedanta Centre
6Lateris Street
Tel Aviv 64166, Israel

Sivananda Yoga Vedanta Centre
c/o Sita Yochi Paz
17 Haportzim Street
Petah Tikwa, Israel

SOUTH AMERICA

Associacion de Yoga Sivananda
Acevedo Diaz 1525 #1
Montevideo,Uruguay

INDIA

Sivananda Yoga Vedanta Centre
37/1929 West Fort, Airport Road
Trivandrum, Kerala 695023, India

Sivananda Yoga Vedanta Nataraja Centre
52 Community Centre
East of Kailash
New Delhi 110 065, India

Sivananda Yoga Vedanta Centre
2 Ranjit Road, Kotturpuram
Madras 600 085, India

Sivananda Yoga Dhanwantari Ashram
P.O. Neyyar Dam, Trivandrum Dist.
Kerala 695 576, India

Sivananda Kutir
Near Siror Bridge
Naitala P.O., U.P.
Himalayas, India

Sivananda Guha
Gangotri Post Office
Gangotri, U.P.
Himalayas, India